*The Sign of
the Flying Goose*

NATIONAL WILDLIFE REFUGE SYSTEM

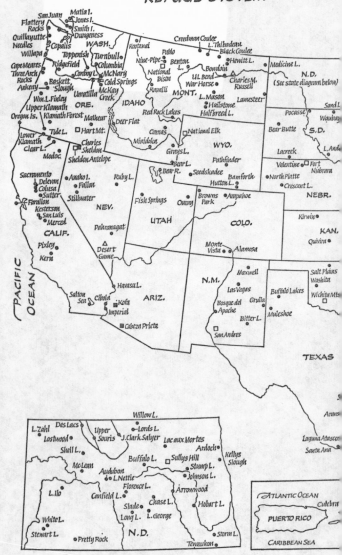

The Sign of the Flying Goose

The Story of the National Wildlife Refuges

Revised Edition

GEORGE LAYCOCK

ANCHOR NATURAL HISTORY BOOKS
ANCHOR PRESS/DOUBLEDAY
GARDEN CITY, NEW YORK
1973

The maps for this book were prepared by the Graphic
Arts Division of The American Museum of Natural
History.

Anchor Books Edition: 1973

The Sign of the Flying Goose was orginally published by
The Natural History Press in 1965. The revised Anchor Books
edition is published with the permission of The Natural History
Press.

To my wife, Ellen,
whose help and encouragement
are reflected in these pages.

Acknowledgments

During the preparation of this book, many people generously shared with me their time and knowledge. The following list includes some of those who deserve my special thanks.

Washington-based administrative employees of the Fish and Wildlife Service: J. Clark Salyer II, Francis C. Gillett, Philip A. DuMont, Gale C. Monson, Carl V. Fermanich and Winston E. Banko.

Regional directors Kenneth F. MacDonald and Walter A. Gresh.

Refuge managers William H. Julian, Jack C. Watson, William D. Wood, Julian A. Howard, Robert D. Jones, Herbert H. Dill, Henry E. Whitley, Robert L. Means, Huyson J. Johnson, Donald V. Gray, Robert C. Twist, Robert F. Russell, Newell B. Morgan and William D. Carter.

Fish and Wildlife Service biologists Ray Glahn, Oscar V. Deming, Arthur F. Halloran, William E. Green, Ged A. Devan, Karl W. Kenyon and Eugene C. Knoder.

Former regional supervisor James Silver; Mrs. J. T. Thompson, daughter of warden Paul Kroegel; Ohio waterfowl biologist Karl E. Bednarik.

Foreword

Our National Wildlife Refuges have been dedicated to the inspiring proposition that Americans should respect and protect all living creatures—and accord them a place in our scheme of values. Through the efforts of such men as Theodore Roosevelt and the late "Ding" Darling this idea has developed into an elaborate system of large and small refuges that provide habitat for nearly all species of wildlife on the North American continent. It is a mark of a higher civilization that America has taken on this obligation with zest and a full appreciation of what wildlife adds to our out of doors.

Our wildlife refuges run the gamut from the eight-million-acre Arctic Wildlife Range in Alaska above the Arctic Circle to small marshes in states like Maine and Florida, and islands in the Hawaiian atoll reserved for the bird life of the Pacific.

This conservation enterprise is as varied—and as fascinating—as the species of birds and animals that inhabit the fifty states.

I encourage all Americans to take advantage of the sheer enjoyment and educational value of this great national resource. Mr. Laycock's book—with its splendid insight into the inner secrets of wildlife ecology—has

given us a much-needed manual which will surely enhance
our interest in this wildlife legacy we all share.

STEWART L. UDALL
Secretary of the Interior

August 4, 1964

Contents

Hectic Decade and
Restless Men

There is no animal on earth big enough, ferocious enough or elusive enough to escape the relentless pressures from the spreading human race. Man proudly fashions his own habitat. He drains and levels the land. He surrounds himself with concrete, steel and manicured fields. He broadcasts chemical poisons that drift in the air and float in the streams and lakes.

Wild species unable to adjust to these changing pressures perish.

Early in the twentieth century a growing concern over the fate of wildlife led to the establishment of our first national wildlife refuge. It was for the most part an event largely unheralded. Few could have visualized the network of wildlife lands that would eventually grow from this small beginning. Today there are more than 300 national wildlife refuges, each marked with a sign bearing the picture of a flying goose, probably the greatest effort any country ever made in wildlife conservation.

Nearly every kind of wild animal known to the fifty states can be found in these areas. Many refuges were set aside especially for hard-pressed waterfowl. But other refuges protect moose, antelope, trumpeter swans, whooping cranes, sea otters, colonial nesting birds, our smallest deer and a host of additional wild creatures. Some of these would almost certainly be extinct were it not for the refuges.

More than eleven million people visit the national wildlife refuges annually. They come to study and photograph the wildlife, to fish, camp, hunt, picnic or explore the outdoors with their families. They may find the boundary of a refuge along a major highway, beside a country lane, deep in a mountain wilderness, or at the edge of the ocean.

For thirty years following its beginning in 1903 the national wildlife refuge program limped along for want of funds. But in the early 1930s there were changes coming for the wildlife refuges. Just ahead lay a period of great activity that would see dozens of new refuges come into existence and would bring to the program new respect and promise. For wildlife, it was about time.

In that third decade of the century, gullied fields were a trade-mark of the hungry times. Depleted forestlands, dried-up wetlands, and Kansas topsoil wind-borne all the way to the Atlantic offered stark testimony of the extent to which men had mistreated natural resources. Drought, drainage and overshooting had brought duck populations to frightening low levels.

Then in January of 1934 President Franklin D. Roosevelt set up a three-man committee, the Beck Committee, on wildlife restoration. Included were publisher Thomas Beck, Aldo Leopold, father of scientific wildlife management, and the famed Iowa cartoonist J. N. Darling. It was Darling who, in the months ahead, would awaken the lethargic Bureau of Biological Survey and set it in motion.

This three-man committee thought big from the beginning. What wildlife, especially waterfowl, needed, said the committee, was fifty million dollars. Who didn't? The economy of the country was still in the doldrums. But at least the extent of the problem was being stated. Then Ding Darling, yielding to the persuasive President and his Secretary of Agriculture, Henry Wallace, agreed to take over as chief of the Bureau of Biological Survey. Now things were about to pop.

Logic told Darling that he had two big needs. The first was money, as much of it as he could corner. It was not until later in the year that the Migratory Bird Hunting Stamp Act would be passed. Any money obtained for wildlife would have to come from congressional appropriations or special funds. Darling quickly became a familiar figure around the Department of Agriculture. Other bureau chiefs up and down the corridors must have viewed the crusading cartoonist with some alarm. They said, "Ding is rattling his tin cup again."

Darling himself admitted that he was using a "straw to suck funds from the other fellow's barrel." Within a few months he had amassed $1 million from a special fund, $1.5 million in land-retirement funds, $3.5 million in drought-relief funds for use only in north-central states, plus $2.5 million in WPA rehabilitation funds. Total, $8.5 million for wildlife. The refuge system had hit the sweepstakes. One catch was that the WPA funds had to be spent before March 31, 1935. There was less than a year to locate, evaluate and acquire $2.5 million worth of wetlands, or see the money revert to other agencies.

Darling's second big need obviously was locating an expert waterfowl biologist who would thrive on work. He thought he knew where he could get such a man. In 1932, as a member of the Iowa State Conservation Commission, he had employed a young, Missouri-born wildlife biologist, J. Clark Salyer II. Darling had been impressed by both the energy and the knowledge of this robust young redheaded outdoorsman.

Born in the river town of Lexington, Missouri, in 1902, Salyer spent much of his youth hunting, fishing, trapping and exploring his grandmother's six-hundred-acre farm. During high school a sympathetic principal often dismissed him from school early to run his trapline through the nearby marshes, where muskrats flourished. In the evenings Salyer ran a second trapline in the uplands for foxes, raccoons, skunks and opossums, and made as much as $750 a year toward his college expenses.

By 1927 Salyer had acquired a B.A. degree in biology at Central College in Fayette, Missouri. He moved on to the University of Michigan and completed work for an M.A. degree in zoology in 1930. When Darling located him again, Salyer was at the University of Michigan. In one more year he would have earned a Ph.D. degree and been ready for a lifetime of teaching biological sciences. But one evening his phone rang.

Darling was not calling from Washington. He was in Ann Arbor. He had an enthusiasm that was contagious and he spoke of the once-in-a-lifetime opportunity someone would now have to accomplish more for waterfowl than anyone before had ever undertaken. Salyer, still determined to complete his education, agreed to take one year's leave from the university and help line up the waterfowl projects.

Desk-bound government workers in the Bureau of Biological Survey hardly saw Salyer before he was gone again. He headed across the country to search out the best waterfowl areas he could find. He consulted with state conservation workers and drew upon the knowledge of experienced field men already employed in the Bureau of Biological Survey.

The days were for working, and Salyer hoarded the hours. He needed time for inspecting lands and planning refuge improvements. The nights were for driving. Each time he eased his foot off the accelerator he could see the remainder of $2.5 million slipping away from the wildlife refuge program. "I saw Mount Shasta in the moonlight four times," he told me, "before I saw it in daylight."

Within six weeks he had driven eighteen thousand miles and drawn up plans for 600,000 acres of new refuge lands. Once the areas were located and approved as potential waterfowl habitat, specialists had to appraise the land and draw up plans for its improvement by the WPA projects. Salyer wore out government cars at a great pace. He drove with his mind on wildlife, and the list of government workers who refused to ride with him grew rapidly. In those months he saw his wife and infant son only on rare occasions.

As his March 31 deadline drew closer, Salyer realized that he and his staff would never make the goal. There was a quarter of a million dollars of the funds he did not have time to spend. Coming that close was viewed as a fantastic accomplishment in Washington. At the last possible moment he climbed into his car amid microscopes, binoculars, clothes and file boxes and swung the nose of the old sedan toward the Potomac.

But Salyer's planning failed to take into consideration a long-established fact of office life. On Saturday at noon doors close and halls become silent until Monday morning. The deadline for Salyer's project would come on Sunday, the last day of March, 1935. When Salyer roared into town on Friday he still had a mountain of paper work to complete. He would then need the signature of the Secretary of Agriculture on wires approving refuge land purchases and projects out in the Dakotas.

With his secretary, Winnie Baun, who had also been secretary for the Beck Committee, Salyer labored far into the night completing the paper work. Early Saturday morning he was back in his office. He stared at the unsigned papers. The Secretary of Agriculture, he had learned, was out of town until Monday morning. Always one to favor the direct course of action, Salyer reached for his pen and signed the authorizations in behalf of the Secretary. "I could have gone to prison," said Salyer. "That was the longest weekend I ever spent."

The first person in line to see the Secretary on Monday morning was J. Clark Salyer. "You came in here to buy land," said Henry Wallace, after hearing Salyer's confession. "Go on back to work."

"It was good," Wallace told me, "that Jay Darling had a man like Salyer to implement his objectives."

As Salyer became more and more involved, he thought

less often about the fact that his year's leave of absence from the university was rapidly disappearing. On December 17, 1934, less than six months after moving to Washington, he became chief of the Division of Migratory Waterfowl.

In the following years he seldom slowed down. Eventually there was not a marsh of more than five thousand acres anywhere in the country he had not seen. He knew every corner of every refuge. He had compiled a priority list of wildlife lands. With the spending of that first $8.5 million rounded up by Darling, plus designation of large segments of public domain, fifty-five new refuge areas had been added to the system.

Through the following years Civilian Conservation Corps camps were established on numerous wildlife refuges. A unique program acquired perpetual easements on thousands of acres of vital waterfowl potholes in the Dakotas. Meanwhile the Migratory Bird Hunting Stamp Act began creating funds earmarked for waterfowl management. In 1936 Congress, urged on by Darling and other conservationists, appropriated six million dollars for more waterfowl restoration work.

Among the fine waterfowl refuges created during this busy decade were Sacramento in California, White River in Arkansas, Mattamusket in North Carolina, Red Rock Lakes in Montana, the Upper Souris and J. Clark Salyer refuges in North Dakota, Swan Lake in Missouri, and Agassiz in northern Minnesota, all of them among the most productive wildlife lands in the country today.

Salyer in his never-ending defense of wildlife refuges left enemies in his path, many of them in other branches of the government service. Let one official or one agency threaten a dollar of wildlife money, and telephones would ring and a grim-faced Salyer would be seen rushing along the corridors to confront the enemy. "You had to howl like a gut-shot panther," he said. "Everybody always had his hand out for a piece of the refuges. You had to know how to say 'no.'"

His pattern of operation as a stormy petrel in government circles was set early. One of the first papers to cross his desk after he became chief of the Division of Migratory Waterfowl was a proposal for the White River National Wildlife Refuge in Arkansas. Salyer knew the area well. The flooded river-bottom timberlands were fabulous puddle-duck wintering grounds. Now a major automobile manufacturer was changing from wood to metal bodies and planning to sell its timber holdings in Arkansas. Salyer thought of the great valuable gum trees growing there, of the thousands of fine oaks, and the hundreds of thousands of ducks. The asking price was $2.75 an acre.

Official papers requesting approval of the deed had been in the office of the Attorney General for what Salyer considered an interminable period. Salyer fretted in disbelief that the government would display this sluggishness in grabbing such a bargain. "Those papers had been gathering dust there," Salyer said, "for three months."

Unable to stand such dalliance any longer, Salyer called the Attorney General's office directly. Shortly he had that Cabinet member on the phone. "I just gave him particular hell," Salyer said.

The conversation had hardly ended before the Attorney General reached the Secretary of Agriculture on the phone. "Who," he asked, "is this new assistant you have over there in refuges?"

The Secretary of Agriculture now called Salyer. "I don't know how you did things out in Michigan," he said, "but here in Washington you don't bawl out the Attorney General of the United States."

In the years that followed Salyer continued to get out of Washington at every opportunity to visit the refuges. One of his superiors recalls that "We could trace his progress across the country by the anguished wails of the regional supervisors."

One refuge manager riding over a refuge in the car behind Salyer's once said, "Look at those arms waving. He's not even driving with his hands. And every time his hand goes out that window it means spending another thousand dollars we don't have."

Even as Clark Salyer grew older, he did not slow down in the pace he set for himself or his employees, not at least until his health forced it. In 1958 his eyesight was failing rapidly. His doctor said it was essential for him to take a month's leave if he were to save his sight. He had been embroiled for months in the struggle to keep the army from carving off a large part of the Wichita Mountains Wildlife Refuge. Now he was even more concerned about a move to open all federal refuges to gas and oil exploration. This, he was certain, was not the time for him to leave. Within a few months he had lost his sight completely. But the Department of the Interior appointed him as adviser and planner on all wildlife work, and his sharp mind and faultless memory still helped guide the Branch of Wildlife Refuges. Salyer had seen the system grow to more than 300 national wildlife refuges.

In 1962 Secretary of the Interior Stewart L. Udall conferred on Salyer the department's Distinguished Service Award. Said the Secretary of the Interior, "His vision, dynamic leadership, loyalty, and dedication to the principles and philosophy of wildlife conservation have given the national wildlife refuge program not only the stature but also the popular public appeal it has today." Shortly afterward, Salyer received the Nash Conservation Award.

The late Ding Darling would have approved. He had written to one of Salyer's long-time and loyal associates a few years earlier, "To me Salyer was the salvation of the duck restoration program of 1934–36. He could make a water analysis in the back end of his battered old automobile. He did most of the work for which I was awarded medals."

In spite of the fact that some of Salyer's fellow workers never felt warmly toward him, I have never known one who did not respect him. "He got a lot of brush down," one of them told me. "That's what we needed in those times, a bulldozer. A nice guy wouldn't have accomplished as much."

In that hectic decade when Salyer first began his career of building the world's greatest system of wildlife refuges, one of his valued assistants was Melvin O. Steen, who later became one of the most capable and respected state conservation-department administrators anywhere. It was Steen who piloted the easement refuge program in the Dakotas and supervised the refuge WPA projects. Steen, like Salyer, possessed the rare quality of stating his thoughts in terse precise language. "Salyer," he told me, "was the best boss I ever had. Sure, he was tough and exacting, but he was also eminently fair and honest. He was the best biologist I have known in my day and his knowledge of American flora and fauna was amazing.

"Salyer was the father, mother and nursemaid of the federal refuge system.

"Vested and predatory interests didn't like him," Steen added, "and for good reason. They couldn't whip him into line. Salyer was a true conservationist. He couldn't be pushed, bribed or intimidated." Steen called Salyer "one of the finest humans I have ever known and one of the best scientists I have known."

From the early giants of conservation in the age of Theodore Roosevelt to the newest refuge worker today, thousands of dedicated people have helped in important ways to shape the national wildlife refuge program. But no individual has ever contributed more to this great conservation effort than J. Clark Salyer II. And it is probable that no one ever will.

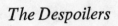

The Despoilers

2

The "Battle of Wichita Mountains" began quietly. Army officers at Fort Sill, Oklahoma, studied their wall maps and plotted their campaign. Their objective was a strip of federal land that lay next door to them. They anticipated no trouble. The land they wanted was only being used for a wildlife refuge. Shortly, a newly proposed bill was dropped into the congressional mill.

"Be it enacted by the Senate and House of Representatives of the United States of America in Congress assembled," said the proposed House Resolution, "that the following described portion of the Wichita Mountains Wildlife Refuge within the State of Oklahoma is hereby transferred to the Department of the Army for military use as part of the Fort Sill Military Reservation, Fort Sill, Oklahoma, without reimbursement or transfer of funds to the Department of Interior." There followed a description of 10,700 acres of this famed wildlife area.

When word flashed across the country, conservationists came out swinging in a fashion that would have done justice to Teddy Roosevelt, who had originally designated the wildlife area in 1905.

Did the army need this land? Did national security depend on it? To conservationists, including some legislators, the whole plan looked like military "empire building." Even before hearings on the proposed bill began before the Subcommittee on Fisheries and Wildlife of the Committee on Merchant Marine and Fisheries, on May 23, 1956, at least five hundred letters had reached Washington arguing against the land transfer.

The records of this hearing were set in type and there are today proofs filed away in Washington archives. But for some reason the testimony was never printed and made available for distribution by the Superintendent of Documents. The army was probably just as happy about this. For one of the few times in its long and noble existence, the U. S. Army was suddenly on the defensive in a battle of its own instigation.

Into the committee hearings came long-time conservation worker Representative John D. Dingell, of Michigan, fighting mad. "I am going to fight this land grab to the last minute of the hearing," he said, "and fight it on the floor as hard as I am able and you can not get six inches of this or any other refuge unless you show me a better case than you have this morning."

Some of the testimony during these hearings is still viewed with disbelief around the halls of Washington. Along with other refuge defenders, most of them in a fighting mood, came J. Clark Salyer II. "We have de-occupied Japan, the Philippines, and much of Germany," stormed Salyer, "but not the refuges." He explained that this refuge had been established to preserve its intrinsic beauty, which approaches national-park caliber, and "to preserve a natural panorama of characteristic animals and their habitat in the great Southwest. Make no mistake about it," the record shows him as testifying, "any land the Army takes over becomes a private hunting club for the higher echelons plus some civilians that play the Army game." To Salyer and other conservationists the very idea that these valued refuge lands should be turned over to the military was unthinkable.

From the Fish and Wildlife Service and several independent conservation organizations came strong testimony.

Only by fighting the hardest kind of battle had the nation's conservationists saved that 10,700 acres for wildlife.

The best the military could do to save face was gain public exclusion from a buffer strip on the refuge where it adjoins Fort Sill.

In a land of such wealth it seems hardly believable that seldom a day passes when a wildlife refuge somewhere in the country is not threatened by forces that would turn out the wildlife. Since the beginning of the refuge program conservationists have fended off many and varied attacks from a wide range of organizations and individuals, and beaten back a steady parade of invaders.

One year before the Battle of Wichita Mountains the air force had surprised conservationists with a bombing plan which would have endangered the remnant flock of whooping cranes where they winter on the Texas coast. This plan called for dropping phosphorous bombs that would have lighted up the night sky for two hundred miles around. The bombs were rated at fifteen million to twenty million candle-power, and each would render a thunderous, ear-splitting explosion. They proposed to test them within half a mile of the whooping cranes' refuge.

There was little question in the minds of bird students about the probable result to the remaining whoopers. The air force had dropped similar bombs over the Salt Plains National Wildlife Refuge in Oklahoma when that area was speckled with 200,000 wintering ducks and 7500 Canada geese. All the physically able waterfowl left with the initial explosion. The skittish whooping cranes would almost certainly depart from the safety of the refuge if the phosphorous bombs were dropped beside them.

Once again word flashed across the country. Letters and wires poured into Washington. Newspapers protested. Canadians, as concerned about the disappearing whooping cranes as anyone, had protected these birds, not only during migration but also on their only nesting grounds. The Canadian government filed a strong protest with the U. S. State Department.

The air force took its bombs elsewhere.

Sometimes the attacks on refuges are both bold and pointless. One of the striking natural features of the Hawaiian Island National Wildlife Refuge had long been a sheer column of rock sticking up from the floor of the ocean in a spire known as Gardner's Pinnacle. Battered and eroded by nature over a millennium, the pinnacle stood as a monument to the elements.

But one morning a navy demolition team was scaling the face of the rock, sticking to its surface like a little group of flies as they inched their way upward. They had sought no permission from the Fish and Wildlife Service, or for that matter even informed them of the scheme. When they were a third of the way from the top they rigged up a string of explosives around this publicly-owned natural wonder, then climbed back down.

A little later there was a thundering explosion. When the rocks and dust had cleared away one third of Gardner's Pinnacle had been blown off. Why? They wanted to use it as a place to land helicopters. No one ever explained what the helicopters would do after they landed up there or why they could not practice landing on some other target.

For decades the irrigator with his plows has been a constant threat to some of the finest of all waterfowl refuges. One of the most famous of these struggles between homesteaders and waterfowl has centered around Tule Lake National Wildlife Refuge in northern California. Agricultural interests have taken parts of this fabulous waterfowl area and still covet the remainder.

The explanation for this conflict is easy enough to see. This refuge and its "across the mountain" neighbor, the Lower Klamath National Wildlife Refuge, were established by nothing more than executive orders from the President's office. And they were established on lands within an irrigation district. The argument through the years has been which should come first, waterfowl or farming.

And because these lands were set aside by executive order, they might be redesignated by another executive order any time the irrigation interests had enough support to force through such a move. What the country's conservationists have long wanted in the Klamath Basin is congressional designation of the refuges, a bill that would clearly state that wildlife gets prime consideration here. Anything less could, in future years, allow destruction of still more of the wetlands. Unless the refuge boundaries can be made firm, there will be continued efforts to kick the ducks from this historic waterfowl region and make room for more potatoes and barley.

The story of Klamath Basin is known almost as well in the halls of Congress as it is in California and Oregon. Bills to correct the situation have come repeatedly before various sessions of Congress. Fortunately there has never been a shortage of able witnesses speaking in behalf of the ducks and geese. For example, at one hearing lifelong professional conservationist C. R. Gutermuth testified in behalf of the Wildlife Management Institute. "It is necessary to glance briefly into the past," he said, "to explain why stabilization of the boundaries of the three refuges is being requested. The wetlands there now encompass virtually all of the waterfowl habitat that remains of the once-vast Klamath Marsh. During the past sixty years," he added, "the water and marsh areas in Tule Lake and Lower Klamath refuges have dwindled from an original 187,000 acres to only 25,000. Despite this tremendous reduction, the refuges provide nesting, resting and feeding habitat for fully 80 percent of the ducks of the Pacific Flyway.

"The Tule Lake problem has been inherited from the past. Successive Secretaries of the Interior have had this situation under continuous review. It has been created and perpetuated by a few irrigation interests that seek to devote every last acre to crop production—average annual yields far below the waterfowl values. The Tule Lake and Lower Klamath refuges have been reduced considerably below their original boundaries.

The strangest of all requests from an agricultural interest was made some years ago by a West Coast food chain which wanted a supply of buffalo meat for its supermarkets. Their request was that the federal government turn over to them all their buffalo for a period of two years so they could found a commercial herd.

Industry and mining interests have frequently looked to the refuges as pockets of riches which they might swoop in and harvest if the wind blew right. One of the most beautiful and productive refuges is Red Rock Lakes in Montana. In this high mountain valley the trumpeter swans were brought back. Some workers in the Branch of Wildlife Refuges never quite forgave the Bureau of Land Management in their own department for permitting a phosphate company to open a pit mine in a pocket of BLM lands above the refuge some years ago. "They took a big bulldozer right up O'Dell Creek," said a Fish and Wildlife Service employee, "and made a road. This let rain and snow wash eighteen inches of silt into Upper Red Rock Lake that first two years."

Next they wanted to run a branch railroad right into the heart of the refuge. Conservation interests managed to block this proposal. But much damage had already been accomplished. "It may take fifty years," I was told, "for the silt to stop washing down off that mountain. It killed a lot of good submerged weed-beds so the emergents, such as cattails and other plants worthless for waterfowl, could come in."

More recently the facts of economic life have been catching up with the two-million-acre Kenai National Moose Range in southern Alaska. This refuge was established in 1941 to protect the largest subspecies of moose in North America, brown bear, Dall sheep, mountain goats and trumpeter swans. Now, deep within this area are oil rigs, villages, school buses and pipelines.

It began with the belief that resting in the earth beneath much of this refuge might be great stores of oil and gas. Oil companies were seeking permission to explore the

Kenai. But the original executive order establishing the refuge had, as later court cases proved, excluded oil exploration.

The oil companies increased their pressure on the Department of the Interior. Perhaps the trend could be curbed by allowing some development on the Kenai moose range. And perhaps this development could be held to rigid regulations worked out between the Branch of Refuges and the oil interests. Maybe it was true, as some oil men claimed, that they could go in and take out the oil without spilling enough to grease a bicycle.

So in 1958 the Department of the Interior relaxed its restrictions against drilling on the Kenai moose range, and opened to exploration more than 90 percent of the substrata certified by the U. S. Geological Survey as having oil-bearing potential. It was an appeasement that many conservationists would soon regret.

The oil people accepted the conditions set forth by the Fish and Wildlife Service and made considerable effort to adhere to the rules. "But they failed," said one wildlife worker, "to inoculate their subcontractors with this thinking." Bulldozers frequently followed the paths of least resistance, including going up the beds of salmon streams in peak spawning periods.

The Department of the Interior was no longer nurturing hope that moose could live among the oil rigs as happily as ever. Gone was the fiction that these were compatible uses of the Alaskan landscape. "Although operations have been carefully controlled," said the Department of the Interior in one report in 1963, "to minimize destructive effects, and the oil companies exhibited a high degree of cooperation, long-term scarring effects to the environment, the disturbance of all wildlife, pollution dangers to fisheries and waterfowl waters, increased fire hazards, and a human occupancy foreign to wildlife habitat have resulted in serious detriment to the range's original objectives."

The story goes on and on. When the Branch of Refuges

began to purchase lands for the Sabine waterfowl refuge on the Gulf Coast of Louisiana, it thought it was buying submarginal land that nobody else wanted. They began their efforts to reclaim it and bring back the grass and wetlands.

"Lo and behold," Salyer exclaimed, "there came an unholy trio of politicians and said they wanted permission to excavate shell beds from beneath the Sabine refuge." Into the purchase of these lands had gone duck-stamp money collected from waterfowl hunters all over the country. Salyer called M. O. Steen, director of the Nebraska Game, Forestation and Parks Commission. Steen, who fully understood the value of refuges, rallied conservationists in the eleven states of the Mississippi Flyway. They made it clear that ducks are a flyway resource, and that what affects ducks in Louisiana just as surely makes its mark on the duck population elsewhere along the flyway. The shell-dredging scheme was blocked.

But the biggest threat to the nation's wildlife refuges may not be the miner, the farmer or the oil prospector, but those who come for fun.

In recent times there has been a great passion in federal and state official circles to create new American playgrounds, to create much-needed new facilities for boating, camping, water skiing, picnics and hunting and fishing. The government has permitted hotels in some of its most scenic regions and ski chair-lifts on its wooded mountainsides. And in many places there can be little argument against these developments—unless the area was intended first of all as a wildlife refuge. Many, if not most, national wildlife refuges provide some recreation possibilities. Recreation on a wildlife refuge is required by law to be secondary to the welfare of the wildlife resources and related to the wildlife of the area.

The family going to the Wichita Mountains wildlife refuge to see the buffalo or prairie dogs can find facilities to picnic, camp or fish while there. But then come multitudes of visitors with no interest in wildlife, demanding ever greater facilities for their comfort and pleasure. Eventually it becomes a "people" refuge.

If you are searching for wildlife areas of great natural beauty which should escape this recreation mania, journey to a settlement called Shellman's Bluff on the coast of Georgia and board a charter boat for the eighteen-mile trip over to Blackbeard Island. I first visited this island in 1959. It was almost as wild and free of man's handiwork as it must have been when Blackbeard was said to have buried his pirate booty here. There were woodlands of pines and great live oaks draped with Spanish moss. Beneath them grew thick tangles of palmettos and greenbrier. On the clean sand beach along the entire eastern edge of the island, mammoth female loggerhead turtles haul themselves out of the sea on warm summer nights to bury leathery-shelled eggs in the sand while tears of undetermined significance roll down their cheeks.

I want to remember this wild island as an untamed seaside habitat where deer slip through the palmettos, wild turkeys feed at the edge of the openings, and great bull alligators roar in the sloughs.

Blackbeard Island is shaped like South America, but it is less than five miles from Surinam to Tierra del Fuego. The roadways we hiked were sandy lanes through the close-growing vegetation. No one lived there except Lawrence Wineland and his wife. Wineland was employed by the Fish and Wildlife Service to protect the refuge. There was a simple boat dock which served quite well for the fishermen and bird students. But there was little else provided. We pitched a tent beneath the pines, cooked our meals on an outdoor fire, and happily did without modern plumbing and fancy gadgets. It was a refreshing experience in a primitive setting.

Blackbeard Island offered one of the few remaining opportunities along the Atlantic Coast to retain an area where wildlife could prosper unmolested by hordes of people, and tomorrow's students could study a coastal island ecology that had retained its natural flavor.

But this refuge, like many another, has felt the recreational pressure. Without question concession stands and modern plumbing will rob picturesque Blackbeard Island of some of its value to wildlife, and to people who cherish the opportunity to visit a wild community still free of man's "improvements."

The suggestions for greater recreation developments come from many quarters, both state and national. We must not forget that wildlife refuges are first of all for wildlife. Theodore Roosevelt did not set Pelican Island aside for picnickers. In fact, trespassers were warned away. As a result the refuge accomplished the task for which it was designated; it helped save an endangered species.

Heavy public use soon strips away the wild character of a refuge area. People are the enemy of wilderness. You will not find wild turkeys among picnickers, terns nesting in the beach-buggy trails, or ducklings hatching in the water skier's wake. On most wildlife refuges we have a simple choice, wildlife and minimum recreation, or we can have full recreational development and minimum wildlife.

*It Began with an Island
for Pelicans*

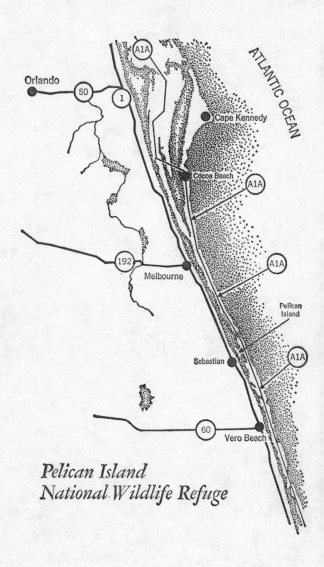

Pelican Island
National Wildlife Refuge

3

On a spring morning in 1903 Paul Kroegel, smoking his pipe as usual, stepped from his house in the village of Sebastian, Florida, and just as he did every morning, stared intently at a little mangrove-covered island out in the mouth of the Indian River. There were several islands out there, all of them outwardly much alike, uninhabited patches of mangrove scarcely higher than the tide.

But one of them in particular merited Kroegel's concentration. On this morning, boat traffic was light on the Intracoastal Waterway which flowed past Sebastian. There was no one near Pelican Island, and this pleased Kroegel. Leave that one to the birds. Let the people go elsewhere.

Sebastian is a quiet old village on the east coast, 135 miles north of Miami on Highway 1, a famous migration route for people headed southward to what they consider a more favorable wintering habitat. Here the Indian River, as it comes to the Atlantic Ocean, spreads out in a broad delta opposite Sebastian. Pelican Island, which Kroegel knew better perhaps than any other man, lay two miles offshore in plain view.

For some reason this was the island, of all those for miles around, most favored by pelicans during the nesting season. But in 1903 Kroegel was openly worried about their future. He had been concerned about the big clumsy-looking birds since he first came to Sebastian.

Kroegel was born in Chemnitz, Germany, and he was only six years old when his mother and sister died. Gotlobb Kroegel promptly gathered up young Paul and headed for America to begin a new life. After living for several years in New York and Chicago, they eventually settled in Florida when Paul was seventeen.

He later explained to his wife and children that the hardships of his childhood strengthened his determination to spend his life working for the things he considered important. High on his list were the wild creatures which he found in such abundance in Florida. Here was a region that drew famous naturalists from all parts of the country. Among those who visited at Kroegel's home in Sebastian over the years were T. Gilbert Pearson, Ernest Thompson Seton, Louis Agassiz Fuertes, Frank M. Chapman and many others who came to paint, photograph or just observe the pelicans on the famous little island. The nesting pelicans provided one of the country's outstanding wildlife spectacles.

"A dense mass of birds had risen at our approach," wrote naturalist Robert H. Lawrence in 1891 in *The Auk*, official publication of the American Ornithologists' Union, "and spread out over the island like a cloud. This great flock was joined by the laggards as we walked about, and the rush and roar of the flapping wings was tremendous, there were hundreds of birds in the air—perhaps a thousand. In tramping about it was difficult to take a dozen steps in any one direction without treading on empty nests, fresh eggs, or young birds."

There was in those times the early awakening of a conservation movement. People were gradually becoming concerned about the welfare of wildlife. The Boone and Crockett Club, of which President Theodore Roosevelt was a member, was working to establish refuges for big-game animals. The Committee on Bird Protection of the American Ornithologists' Union, and a few years later The Audubon Society, were searching for ways to bring protection to many of Florida's larger birds, including the brown pelicans. In spite of the Florida legislature's action in 1901 prohibiting the killing of almost all birds excepting game birds, there was still widespread slaughter, much of it for no purpose.

The pelicans on the island opposite Kroegel's home were being especially hard hit. The American Ornithologists' Union tried to buy the island, but discovered that it was unsurveyed government property. Then they decided to hire Kroegel as a special warden to protect the pelicans as best he could.

The pelican warden's physical stature was hardly enough to frighten poachers and vandals away from the island. He stood only five feet, six inches tall and weighed a scant 135 pounds.

In spite of the fact that he had practically no authority to back him up, Kroegel was heroic in the pelican's defense. He detested those who shot the birds simply to see them fall. He never understood why wealthy vacationers going to Palm Beach on their yachts considered it sport to fire into the flocks of slow-flying pelicans. If Kroegel knew in time that they were coming, he would run to his little sailboat and race for the island. Given favorable winds he might get there before the yacht came abreast, and the gunners would see between them and the birds a grim-looking man standing in his boat with a menacing double-barreled shotgun cradled in his arms. But when it was calm or the wind was against him Kroegel often arrived too late to do anything but destroy the cripples.

Meanwhile conservationists were working to have Pelican Island set aside as a government bird refuge. The fact that it was already government property made this seem logical. The American Ornithologists' Union recommendation on this eventually worked through government channels to the desk of the President. There were those who said the President would be overstepping his authority. Where was the precedent for establishing a federal bird refuge? But with a characteristic bold stroke the President signed his name to the document. *"It is hereby or-*

*dered that Pelican Island in Indian River in section nine,
township thirty-one south, range thirty-nine east, State of
Florida, be, and it is hereby reserved and set apart for the
use of the Department of Agriculture as a preserve and
breeding ground for native birds."*

THEODORE ROOSEVELT

The date was March 14, 1903. Now Paul Kroegel, com-
missioned by the President of the United States to watch
over Pelican Island, had full authority for the first time to
protect the bids. Kroegel's pay was fifteen dollars a
month—out of which he furnished his own boat, and later,
when he used a motor launch, his fuel as well. Most of
his living still came from the boat shop he operated in
Sebastian.

Warden Kroegel had no way of knowing on this spring
morning that he was making history. He walked briskly
down to the dock where he kept the *Yellow Kid,* a fast little boat from his own shop. Shortly, with the breeze filling
her sail, the *Yellow Kid* slipped across the mouth of the
river toward Pelican Island.

On the island Kroegel nailed a sign well above the high-
tide mark for all to see. There would be no mistaking the
meaning of the message he had lettered, "U. S. Reservation—Keep Off."

Even though the new warden had posted his sign on
the mangroves there were still those who preferred to dis-
regard the law. It was no longer easy, however, to disre-
gard the warden. With his appointment the government
had given Kroegel a new flag and a fifty-foot flagpole. Instead of putting the flag on Pelican Island, Kroegel
mounted it outside his home in Sebastian. From this point
the flag was in plain view of boat captains as they rounded
the bend. Captains saluted the flag with a blast of the whistle and gave Kroegel ample warning that the boat was
headed toward Pelican Island. On weekends and holidays
there was seldom a meal in the Kroegel home when the

warden didn't have to jump up from the table and race out to stand guard over the pelicans.

"When diplomacy and dignified authority were ignored," warden Kroegel's daughter, Mrs. J. T. Thompson, has told me, "he reached for his double-barreled ten-gauge shotgun, which he always carried in his boat, and chased the invaders away from the area. He considered the surrounding waters within gun range of Pelican Island," she added, "to be the boundaries of the refuge."

But despite the existence of the new refuge and the best efforts of the pelicans' friends, the birds made no startling recovery in numbers. Late in October of 1910, a roaring hurricane swept the coast of Florida. Naturalist George Nelson, who spent much of his time out there with the pelicans during those eventful years, wrote later in *The Auk* that, "The river rose and completely submerged the Island, driving the young to the more elevated islands near by." The island was flooded for more than three weeks following the hurricane.

Meanwhile the adult pelicans returned to start a new nesting season. Their island was now submerged, so they moved on and built their nests on a larger island four hundred yards to the southeast. When the water went down the birds chose to stay on the new island, which Kroegel named "New Pelican Island."

To the human eye this looked like an ideal location for pelicans to nest. Half of it was densely wooded with large black mangroves. There were five thousand pelican nests on the island that season. But on the following June 15, hordes of mosquitoes descended on the island. They attacked the pelicans in such numbers that the birds abandoned their nests and the young in them. George Nelson speculated that the mangroves served as a windbreak to prevent the wind from blowing the mosquitoes off as it had on the more open Pelican Island. Perhaps the pelicans had shifted their nesting from island to island for thousands of years. They still do. The island they occupy this year may be abandoned next.

Pelicans build bulky nests of sticks on the ground or in the mangroves and lay two or three white eggs. Once these have hatched they raise their young on a strict diet of fish.

The pelican's food habits have always made this bird unpopular among commercial fishermen reluctant to share the riches of the sea with a bird noted for being a mighty fisher. It is hard for fishermen to believe, as scientific investigation has proved, that the pelican's diet tends largely to fish of scant commercial value. He is, after all, four and a half feet long, has a wingspread of more than six feet, and can dive headlong into the ocean to come up with his great beak holding a bulk order of fish.

During the years of the First World War, in the heat of a national emergency, the pelican's enemies tried again to accomplish what they had started long before the bird had a refuge of its own. "These birds," claimed the commercial fishermen, "are seriously depleting the human food supply." They advocated complete destruction of the remaining pelicans and insisted that the fish resources off the Florida coast were but a fraction of what they had been in previous years. They overlooked the fact that the pelican populations had also dwindled to a remnant of what they had once been. And they ignored the evidence that when white men came here both fish and pelicans were abundant. They granted interviews to newspapers and enlisted the support of a few politicians to bring on a full investigation of the pelican's diet by the Food Administration. The argument grew so serious that the Florida Audubon Society in 1918 published a pamphlet called *A Defense of the Pelican*.

Naturalist Frank M. Chapman warned that, "The colonial nesting habits of pelicans would make it possible practically to eliminate them in a season." Then he pointed out that "these birds feed chiefly on inedible fish, like menhaden." Even warden Paul Kroegel got into the fray with one of his rare public statements. He insisted that the reduced catches were caused primarily by the commercial fisherman's own greediness, and added that they never hesitated to break a law.

One dark night during this controversy, a group of commercial fishermen put their young sons ashore on Pelican Island. They clubbed to death hundreds of the birds. It was the only such disaster to befall the pelicans in all the years of warden Kroegel's watch over them. Sadly, the warden went about the island the following day dispatching those pelicans too badly crippled to recover. The boys were tried and found guilty. They were released to the custody of their parents but never again was there the threat of such an action against the pelicans. Even in the trying times of national emergency the pelican kept his legal protection.

For sixty years after warden Kroegel nailed up his refuge sign, our first national wildlife refuge was commonly described as a "three-acre island off the east coast of Florida." Then came a series of developments which dusted off some little-known facts about this refuge and revealed that actually it was more than a single three-acre island.

Kroegel's widow had carefully preserved the warden's set of lantern slides. One day in 1963 William Julian, then refuge manager of all the south Florida national wildlife refuges, was looking through these old lantern slides and one suddenly attracted his attention. Standing out plainly in it was a refuge sign that said, not "Pelican Island," but "New Pelican Island."

Julian dug back into the records and found that on January 26, 1909, six years after signing the first order, President Roosevelt had taken another look at the pelican situation and promptly enlarged the refuge to include "all small islands within sections 9 and 10." Now there were actually four pelican islands where, as the President wrote, "It is unlawful for any person to hunt, trap, capture, willfully disturb or kill any bird of any kind whatever or take the eggs of such birds within the limits of this reservation."

Julian promptly forwarded a letter to his superiors in the Regional Office of the Fish and Wildlife Service in Atlanta,

Georgia. He was eager to get out there and post all the designated islands.

Meanwhile, however, other events were unfolding in the background. A group of Miami speculators had petitioned the county commissioners for approval of a plan to extend a bulkhead into the mouth of the Indian River north of Pelican Island, the beginning of a housing development that would certainly threaten the pelicans. And government workers were busy determining the exact boundaries of this historic refuge.

Lined up against the Miami speculators were the always alert Florida Audubon Society and a new organization formed specifically to protect the wildlife area, the Indian River Area Preservation League. Once more the friends of the pelicans won. On December 5, 1963, the Federal Land Register officially detailed the boundaries of the enlarged Pelican Island National Wildlife Refuge. The refuge now covers 756 acres. Julian, just as had Paul Kroegel in 1903, went about erecting refuge signs around the newly determined limits of the refuge. This time it was the familiar sign of the flying goose.

Warden Kroegel had been in charge of Pelican Island until 1919. An economy-minded government, seeking places to cut costs after the war, decided the federal government could no longer afford a guard over Pelican Island. So they retired warden Kroegel, first of the long list of people who would eventually work on national wildlife refuges. Kroegel died in Sebastian in 1948 at the age of eighty-four.

In November 1963 the refuge he had so vigorously protected became the first wildlife area to be designated by the National Park Service as a national historical monument. The dedication was conducted in Sebastian, where Kroegel had arrived eighty-two years earlier. At the same time, local citizens decorated the pelican warden's grave with a special plaque while his widow, daughter, son and grandson looked on.

Pelican Island, first of the national wildlife refuges, had

become more than a safety zone for harassed birds. Here the government of the United States first indicated its willingness to set aside, for all time, a bit of its land to protect wildlife from the advance of people. It was an unheralded beginning for what would someday become one of the greatest systems of wildlife refuges anywhere in the world.

Alligator Country
Okefenokee

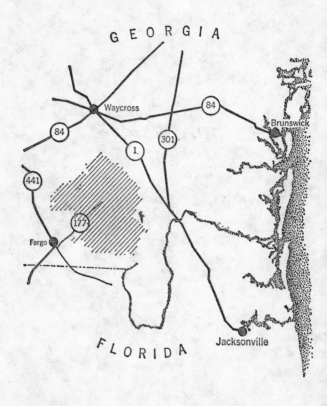

Okefenokee National Wildlife Refuge

4

The big mallard flying in from the northeast dropped lower and lower in the autumn sky as the edge of the swamp came into view. The swamp stretched out in front of him and to both sides now as far as he could see. Highways, farms and towns with their buildings and people were left behind. Below was only the vast solitude of the sprawling Southern swamp. The old greenhead, flying no more than a hundred yards above the highest cypress trees, held his course.

Stripped now of most of their summer foliage, the cypress, draped with gray-green Spanish moss, stood out against the dark swamp water. For mile after mile out through the swamp, their formation was broken only by occasional patches of pine marking the islands.

The drake flew steadily over islands, open lakes, small saturated floating bogs and shallow marshlands. He crossed the "prairies" which, in Okefenokee, are open waters matted with water lilies, "neverwets" and swamp marigolds.

He kept a straight course, as if he knew exactly where he was headed. He ignored the ducks on Dinner Pond calling to him and other passing strangers. He crossed over Minnie's Island, then Billy's Island, where Billy Bowlegs, the Seminole war chief, once hid with his people.

Beyond Honey Island the big greenhead circled once

and almost settled in among the ducks on Honey Island Prairie. But he traveled on, almost to the edge of the swamp, until he came to the sprawling Grand Prairie off to the east of Black Jack Island. He gave a single answering call to the ducks below, circled and began slipping air off his wings to settle in fast. There was a ripple where his outstretched feet braked his descent. His journey was finished. Shortly he was lost among hundreds of other mallards, black ducks and ringnecks that had come to winter in Okefenokee.

For forty miles north of the Florida-Georgia border and twenty-five miles from east to west, Okefenokee, perhaps the world's most spectacular swamp, stands like an unyielding stranger in a land of cotton patches and piney woods. Okefenokee, more than a single scene, is a panorama. And, more than a wildlife community, it is a whole complex of communities. Incredibly rich in wildlife, this is a fascinating and mysterious land to everyone who visits it.

The true mystery of Okefenokee is that it still exists at all, that it has not been cleared of its timber, drained of its water and patched over with farms, highways and subdivisions. Men have tried their best to accomplish all these. But Okefenokee is as stubborn and resistant as it is beautiful and mysterious.

Unlike the typical swamp, Okefenokee is not a low-lying region into which waters drain from the surrounding area. In fact, this swamp is a source of water, the birthplace of two rivers.

The average level of Okefenokee is no more than 130 feet above the Atlantic, of which, in ancient times, it was a part. Across the swamp, from north to south, extends Trail Ridge. This low ridge is Okefenokee's Great Divide. Waters that fall on the west of the ridge flow off to the Gulf of Mexico down the Suwanee River, which drains most of Okefenokee and has its origin here. But waters falling to the east of the divide flow slowly down the twisting boat runs to become the St. Marys River, which empties into the Atlantic forty-five miles away. Okefenokee water comes both from rainfall and from innumerable springs. These waters, strained through the acid peat bogs, are, natives say, pure enough to drink.

There are islands in Okefenokee that are nothing more than floating masses of vegetation. On windy days they may drift across the lake, and the island you saw in the morning may be gone in the evening. And with it are gone the animals living on it and the fish living beneath it. These floating islands grow as vegetation builds up on them. Sooner or later trailing roots of the floating plants get a purchase on the bottom, and the wandering island is anchored in place. Its soil builds in depth until broad-leaved trees or cypress can grow there. To the Okefenokee swamp people these hammocks are "houses," the houses of alligators, bobcats, raccoons and water birds.

The Indians, the first men to live in the swamp, changed it little. They hunted and fished here and later hid from the white men who pursued them. In the 1830s the Seminoles took refuge on the islands deep inside Okefenokee, and from this base they slipped out into the surrounding countryside to make raids on the white man's property. These Seminole escapades enraged the white community, and challenged the military authority of the War Department in Washington. But many a white man thought that the Seminoles, protected by the unknown that lurked deep within Okefenokee, could not be routed.

Then the War Department handed the assignment to a tough Georgia-born professional soldier, General Charles Floyd. The general, on November 11, 1838, with 250 dragoons, splashed and slashed his way into the swamp from the south edge near the present site of Fargo, Georgia. Following the Seminoles' own trails the soldiers routed the Indians from Okefenokee, destroyed their village and marched out of the swamp again, to the relief of the settlers and the military minds in Washington. The Seminoles found refuge in Florida, while in Okefenokee, the fast-growing aquatic vegetation quickly covered and obliterated most evidence of the Indians and the brief campaign that evicted them.

With the Indians cleared from the swamp, a few white families gradually moved in. They built cabins on the larger islands. They cleared fields and grew enough corn for the family table, the mules, and the whisky stills, and took the rest of their livelihood from the swamp. They poled their shallow-draft boats through the dark swamp, fishing and hunting. Egrets were sometimes taken for their plumes, alligators were relentlessly hunted for their hides, and the pine trees were slashed for turpentine. But seed was left and these scars could be healed. Meanwhile, outside the swamp, ambitious men were looking more frequently toward Okefenokee. The time was approaching for a showdown between persistent men and the resistant swamp. What could man do with this vast area of cypress, egrets, and alligators? He could, as he was steadily doing in other places, bend nature to his will, conquer Okefenokee, and translate its riches into dollars.

The first man to tackle this gigantic engineering challenge seriously was Captain Harry Jackson, a lawyer from Atlanta. He had energy and vision, and his father, General Henry R. Jackson, had money to back him. What they proposed, with the full blessing of Georgia's governor and its general assembly, was a simple, direct approach: drain Okefenokee.

The idea was highly popular around Georgia in 1890. Harvest the timber. Reclaim the farmland. Change the face of the earth. Progress! So, on January 1, 1891, the governor granted to Jackson's Suwanee Canal Company 15,000 acres in land lots plus 219,000 unsurveyed acres of Okefenokee, and the wheels of progress were in motion. But in the years ahead the wheels were to creak and groan.

Captain Jackson began his digging from Camp Cornelia on the eastern side, and his ditch, which is still used by fishing boats, eventually reached fourteen miles into the heart of the swamp. Millions of dollars went into digging Jackson's canal, but fourteen miles, by the captain's own reasoning, was only a beginning. By the time the sources of money had dried up, Okefenokee was still as wet as ever. In fact, it was a little wetter because numerous springs, newly opened by the ditching, fed additional water into the swamp. Some people even began to think the canal was draining water from the St. Marys River backward into the swamp. This idea, in spite of the fact that it was not so, gave the canal a name that stuck; it was called Jackson's Folly. When the canal was eventually abandoned, Okefenokee had won another round and had suffered little more than the loss of some slash pine from the higher spots around Camp Cornelia.

Next, Okefenokee faced its biggest threat of all, and one that came closer than any other in its history to destroying it. The Suwanee Canal Company sold its Okefenokee holdings, which now totaled 257,889 acres, to the Hebard Lumber Company of Philadelphia.

In that year of 1900, Okefenokee still stood rich in timber, water and wild creatures. No one, in fact, even knew the extent of the timber resources inside the swamp. The Hebards wanted to know more about the cypress, black gum and pine they had purchased and they asked their Georgia real-estate agent, R. R. Hopkins, to find a man who could spend a month running lines through the swamp.

Almost immediately Hopkins thought of his nephew, young John Hopkins, a bushy-haired, pipe-smoking outdoorsman who had recently opened his first law office in the sleepy county-seat town of Darien. John was always ready to go on a duck hunt or tramp the piney woods with a pack of hound dogs. In spite of his love for the outdoors, if anyone had asked him or if he himself had given it articulate thought, he would doubtless have said that he expected to go right on reading the law for the rest of his life. The promise of a month in the big swamp, however, was more than he could resist. And when that month was finished the lumber company asked him to stay a second month.

Okefenokee gets a grip on a man. It has happened with
settlers who lived inside the swamp, and with visiting naturalists who returned time and again to study the strange
wilderness. And it happened to John Hopkins. He stayed
in the swamp, working at various jobs, for forty-five years.
He came closer to conquering Okefenokee than any other
man ever had, only to find eventually that the swamp
would convert him into one of its stanch defenders.

First he ran survey lines through the swamp. Two men
dragged a hundred-foot steel measuring chain, while another workman with machetes helped clear a trail. The
chainmen began in Chase Prairie, working first from boats,
then by wading through the waist-deep waters, putting
egrets and cranes to flight and disturbing reluctant alligators. Said Hopkins, "The forward chainman sometimes
showed but little above the water."

Lines were run and the swamp was measured. Later
the timber was estimated. Now the owners were ready to
cut the cypress, pines and gum trees and haul them out of
the swamp to a sawmill which Hopkins built at Waycross.

Hopkins' crews also drove pilings through the swamp's
ooze and muck, down into firm sand. On them they built
a narrow-gauge railroad. And for two decades the rattling
of the woodpeckers and the bellowing of the 'gators mingled with the ring of the ax and the splash of giant cypress
trees falling into the swamp. Car after car of fine timber
came out of the heart of Okefenokee behind the chugging
cabbage-head locomotive.

But even after the lumbering operations ceased in 1926,
there were still remote stands of virgin swampland timber
and wildlife communities that had not yet been destroyed.
Visiting naturalists, fishermen and ordinary curious citizens took a growing interest in Okefenokee. The Georgia
Assembly had declared Okefenokee a game reservation in
1919. Meanwhile, the U. S. Biological Survey, predecessor
of the Fish and Wildlife Service, was enlarging its system
of national wildlife refuges. Between March 9 and 14, in
1931, the U. S. Senate Special Committee on Conserva-

tion of Wildlife Resources made an inspection trip into Okefenokee. With them went John Hopkins.

The Senate committee decided, "That this immense area is not of primary value for migratory bird refuge purposes." More than waterfowl alone was involved here, however. Okefenokee was the historic home of a complex community of plants and animals of many kinds. Consequently, the Senate committee added this note to its recommendations: "However, Okefenokee is unique in many ways and would make an attractive and valuable sanctuary for all forms of wildlife indigenous to this region."

Next, timber specialists from the U. S. Forest Service, working with Hopkins, ran a timber cruise of parts of the swamp. The Biological Survey could now make an offer to the Hebard Lumber Company. The area known as Okefenokee National Wildlife Refuge came into government possession at midnight on November 30, 1936. The price was $1.50 an acre, about $400,000. An executive order from President Franklin D. Roosevelt officially established Okefenokee National Wildlife Refuge on March 30, 1937. The refuge includes four fifths of the swamp and covers 330,973 acres.

Work began almost immediately. Where trees had been sawed down and hauled off, they were now protected. Birds and reptiles and mammals were now offered protection from poachers. The Biological Survey needed people to protect and rebuild the swampland, so they turned to men who understood it. The first patrolmen were two native Okefenokee residents, Sam Mizell and Jesse B. Gay. They knew every turn and twist in the swamp and understood the creatures, wild and human, they might encounter there. A few months later the refuge was assigned its first refuge manager. He also was a man who knew Okefenokee, John Hopkins. He held that job for the next eight years, "protecting," as he said, "the forests I had disturbed and the wildlife I had pursued."

Meanwhile, Civilian Conservation Corps crews were sent to Okefenokee. At Camp Cornelia, once the site of

Harry Jackson's ill-fated canal, service buildings went up. Miles of single-strand fence were built around the boundaries, and the sign of the flying goose helped mark the refuge area.

Okefenokee had given up 40 percent of her timber. More had been slashed for turpentine. But the scars are healing. With a couple of exceptions, the plants and animals that once lived there are still there. The cougar is gone. So, perhaps, is the ivory-billed woodpecker. Or, as some suspect, remnant numbers of the great woodpecker may still live deep within Okefenokee. During his early days in Okefenokee, Hopkins saw ivory-billed woodpeckers several times, once, "within a few yards." But he never saw them after 1903.

The big, noisy pileated woodpeckers, champion woodcutters of the swamps, are abundant in Okefenokee. So are the fur bearers. Hopkins used to keep an informal record of the fur trade in Okefenokee when the Hebards owned the swamp. "There were some years," he said, "when 150 to 200 people took furs or 'gator skins from Okefenokee." They sold to local buyers or shipped directly to outside cities as many as 10,000 raccoons, 200 otters, 25 or more bobcats, a few skunks and as many as 2000 alligator skins in a year.

The black bears of Okefenokee, before the days of the refuge, lived under the perpetual threat of the farmer's gun. You couldn't blame the bear for killing a farmer's pig and you couldn't blame the farmer for killing the bear. And even if you could blame him for killing the bear, it would seem inhuman, in those lean years before television, to deny him the chase. A bear hunt could bring Okefenokee neighbors together in high spirits any time.

Plows stopped and mules stood in their harness. The long gun came down from the pegs above the cabin door, the lean hound dogs loped in to the whoop and holler and the bear soon knew he was in trouble. If the bear took to the wet prairies, the swamp hunters could outdistance him in their pole boats, and often head him toward a waiting neighbor.

But let the bear make it to the cypress bays, where moss, smilax and "hoorah bushes" grew so thick they cut out the sun's light, and he could push through the jungle faster than his hunters. Chase him long enough, and hard enough, however, and the bear might tree. And the farmer added a new story to his repertoire of bear-hunting tales.

This is a region incredibly rich in frogs, toads, turtles and snakes. There are twenty species of frogs and toads to keep the swamp awake on a summer night. Okefenokee is alive with turtles in twelve varieties. Soft-shelled turtles are everywhere. The Florida terapin, known around Okefenokee as the "hard-backed cooter," lines the sunning logs in midday. The evil-tempered alligator snapper, sometimes weighing one hundred pounds, lies camouflaged on the muck bottoms of the lakes. When hungry he opens his clamp-like jaws and lets his tongue move in the current until some unsuspecting fish mistakes it for a worm and swims squarely into the jaws of death.

There are twenty-eight species of snakes in the swamp, most of them non-poisonous. If you wander through Okefenokee long enough you may meet a rattler. You are more likely to encounter the cottonmouth moccasin, the most abundant of the swamp's poisonous snakes. Even so, they do not, as some imagine, crawl on every limb. Said one naturalist who spent long weeks in Okefenokee, "I have seldom seen more than two or three cottonmouths in the course of a month."

Okefenokee's bird list includes 225 species. Graceful swallow-tailed kites, the barred owls and the osprey patrol the land and water. The prothonotary warbler nests in the hollow cypress knees. The pileated woodpecker dips and soars through the woodlands trailing behind him his raucous notes. The heavy-winged Florida crane lives there with the white ibis, the common egret and the anhinga. And the mockingbird sings the songs of all of them, then copies the call of the pinewoods tree toad for an encore.

The mallards and black ducks come to spend the winter. And with them come the ringnecks and pintails. Wood ducks live here the year around. "Okefenokee," says the U. S. Fish and Wildlife Service, "has considerable value as a migratory waterfowl refuge." The ducks no longer come in the multitudes enjoyed by Suwanee Canal Company workmen who, according to one report, "shot until their guns got too hot, or they had all they wanted." This is not the fault of Okefenokee, but the grim story of the ducks everywhere in a world where they are pressed increasingly by human competition.

Of all the creatures in Okefenokee, however, alligators dominate the scene. While the days are gone when "You could walk across Billy's Lake on the 'gator backs," there are still more than five thousand alligators in Okefenokee. The poaching has been all but stopped and the big reptiles live abundantly on the wild meat around them.

Poachers once cut deeply into the 'gator's ranks. There was a time when the landing at Billy's Island reeked with the odor of decaying alligator flesh and the bones were stacked high. Hunters, poling their boats through the prairies at night, would shine their lights around the edges of the 'gator holes. An alligator's eyes shine like twin rubies in a spotlight, and a rifle bullet between them would bring another hide to the market.

How big do alligators get? Early explorers told of taking aging 'gators that measured twenty feet and weighed half a ton. But seldom is a wild one found now that would measure more than twelve feet long.

To one side of her den the female alligator builds a mound of grass to receive her eggs, which are white and about the size of a hen's egg. They are deposited in layers and covered with vegetation, to be warmed by the sun until they hatch. Nearby the watchful female guards her treasure, but often not well enough. Many of her eggs are found and eaten by the elusive raccoon and the wandering bear.

But from the eggs that escape the predator's raids come

a fresh crop of young that measure eight inches in length and weigh less than two ounces each, a morsel for anything that can catch them. And many creatures of the swamps can. In spite of the careful guarding by the old female, some of her young go to feed the turtles, raccoons, owls and their own cannibalistic father.

By the time the young alligator is a year old he may weigh only a half pound, hardly a fair match for many of the creatures around him. But the older an alligator gets, the safer he becomes. He may weigh fifteen pounds by the time he is three years old, and by the time an alligator is six years old he has matured. He has established his home territory and no doubt defended it successfully against other alligator invaders.

In Okefenokee, life for the alligators goes on, year after year, much as it did before the white man came with his ax and his rifle and his never-ending compulsion to drain what is wet and then irrigate what is dry.

With poaching controlled and timber harvest halted, the great swamp is still threatened by drought and fire. Historic records show that fires come with the dry years and that droughts hit the Okefenokee country about once every twenty-two years.

What does a dry year do to the swamp? Much of Okefenokee is under less than three feet of water. The big drought of 1954 and 1955 lowered the water level four feet. The prairies dried up, the alligator holes were no longer under water, and the 'gators wandered through the swamp looking for places to live. The shore birds and waterfowl went elsewhere to feed. Fish, amphibia, and millions of other creatures perished. Then lightning and wildfire hit the tinder-dry woodlands and began to burn the peat beds, which go down to twenty feet in some places. Smoke choked the swamp for many weeks.

A certain amount of fire, to the surprise of many, can help prolong the life of a swamp such as Okefenokee. Said one biologist before a congressional committee studying Okefenokee, "If fires did not lower the swamp floors periodically, it would build up above the water and above the rim of the basin and would drain itself within a hundred years or less."

But outside the swamp, farm drainage ditches were drawing off some of the surface waters that drained through Okefenokee. And heavy demands on the ground water were gradually lowering the water table through that section of Georgia and Florida. So in the late 1940s the Fish and Wildlife Service began searching for a way to hold more of the water inside the swamp, especially in dry years. To accomplish this they built a low dam, or sill, across the Suwanee where it leaves the wildlife refuge. This structure, plus constant and unrelenting fire patrols, has helped once more to stabilize Okefenokee.

This magnificent swamp has always had strong appeal for visitors. The Fish and Wildlife Service, realizing this, has provided ways for bird watchers, fishermen, photographers and boaters to get into the swamp.

The public may enter the swamp at three places, the north, east and west entrances. Seven miles down Highway 1, south of Waycross, Georgia, is a hard-surfaced road into Okefenokee Swamp Park. This is the north entrance, and the place where tourists can in an hour or two get a good idea of what Okefenokee is like. The park covers twelve hundred acres of Cowhouse Island. It is operated by a non-profit organization that leases the land from the State of Georgia.

There is a small zoo here with typical animals of Okefenokee, the otter, raccoon, alligator, egret and bobcat among others. By boats, or by a long boardwalk leading to a sight-seeing tower, visitors can see a section of Okefenokee without getting swamp water on their street shoes.

Fishermen go into the swamp by the east entrance (out of Folkston to Camp Cornelia) or by the west entrance (at Camp Stephen Foster from Fargo). The federal government has licensed concessionaires at each of the entrances to provide supplies, boats and motors of less than ten horsepower to those who do not bring their own.

Inside the swamp the Okefenokee visitor must be accompanied by a guide. Fishing is done according to the laws of Georgia and with that state's licenses—except that fishing is limited to daylight hours and live fish are prohibited as bait. Regulations forbid visitors bringing in firearms or unleashed dogs.

Fishing Okefenokee is a memorable experience. On one trip there two of us fished with Will Cox, who for many years was chief guide at Okefenokee Swamp Park. He had lived all his life in the swamp.

We eased eventually into a large 'gator hole and in the oppressive heat of a summer afternoon we did not raise a single bass. But this, considering the time of day, was no surprise, and we soon gave it up to try the idea Will Cox suggested. "A man," he said, "can get whatever he needs from the swamp." With his thin-bladed pocketknife, he cut into the stem of a water lily and extracted a white grub. He rigged it on a hook and tossed it back as far as he could under the moist edge of a floating island. In less than a minute he brought a fine warmouth bass into the boat. We took one every time we tried this bait. And later in the evening, as the sun set, we also took a few husky largemouth bass on top-water plugs.

Okefenokee is not simply a refuge for waterfowl or alligators, fur bearers or wading birds. It is a complete wilderness community, a refuge for everything wild. Here Nature is permitted to balance her own books. How much the 'gators prey on the ducks, the woodpeckers consume the carpenter ants, or the crows rob the ibis nest is not really important. These are natural forces. The prey can withstand the predation and live, in turn, to prey on something else.

But when man invades this wild community the scales tip. Most of the time man himself does not fully understand what harm he creates by destroying wild habitat and obliterating a wilderness. Then sometimes he does—as, for example, he did eventually in Okefenokee. This "Land of the Trembling Earth" was saved just in time. In time for the 'gators, bears, ducks and cranes, and for those among us who like to see them, hear them, or just know they are out there as they were a thousand years ago, among the cypress and the pines.

*Islands That Belong
to Animals*

Arctic Ocean

CANADA

ALASKA

Anchorage

Gulf of
Alaska

Kodiak Island

Bering Sea

Alaska Peninsula

Aleutian Islands

Aleutian Islands
National Wildlife Refuge

5

In June 1741 Captain-Commander Vitus Bering left the shores of Siberia to cross the uncharted sea. A few months later he had reached the coast of Alaska, fabulous northern land of unfathomed secrets, unexplored space and strange creatures not seen before by white men. But Vitus Bering, a Danish navigator in the service of the Russian Navy, was in for trouble.

He had started with two ships, the *St. Peter* and *St. Paul,* and shortly after sailing the ships had separated. Bering, in the *St. Peter,* was eventually cruising along that chain of islands that reach southwestward from the southern coast of Alaska. One thing about this region that disturbed Bering and his crew was the fog, thick as borsch and seldom lifting.

The native Aleuts in their scattered settlements along those islands could have told Bering about the fogs where the warm Japan Current meets the cold Oyoshio Current out of the seas to the north. Much of the year intermittent fog and rain are constant elements of Aleutian Islands weather. Skies are gray, seas are turbulent, and a biting wind that sometimes seems to rise out of nowhere whips the stinging rain with relentless force. The mountainous and treeless islands, born of volcanoes, rise gray and stark out of the sea. The islands in this "chain" are emergent peaks of a partially submerged range of mountains. This island realm of teeming wildlife has fascinated white men since they first saw it in that year of 1741.

The Aleutian Islands lie at the north border of the Pacific Ocean and the south edge of the Bering Sea. They stretch for eleven hundred miles in a great arch of stepping stones from the Alaska Peninsula toward Asia. The archipelago ends at Attu. There are some two hundred major islands in the group. Seventy of them are named.

Aleutian Islands weather is mild by northern standards. It is free of the bitter cold known to the interior of Alaska. There is snow, sometimes a foot or more deep, but it is often wet and slushy. On the higher mountain slopes, of course, snows are deeper and temperatures lower. But at the lower elevations the thermometer seldom drops more than ten or fifteen degrees below freezing, even in midwinter. One set of weather records covering parts of the Aleutians for an entire year showed temperatures ranging as high as sixty-nine degrees in August and down to seven in February. Of the 365 days, only fifteen were completely clear.

This kind of information Vitus Bering was gathering the hard way. Then on a typical foggy November day, the famous explorer had to face the truth; he was lost. The *St. Peter* ran aground in the shallows. She shuddered and with sickening noises rammed against the sharp volcanic rocks. The survivors splashed ashore on an uninhabited island and began looking about for sources of food to carry them through the approaching winter.

Before long they were busy catching big sea otters, which had been unknown to them before they came to these islands. The animals, hundreds of them, drifted idly on their backs in the kelp beds or played and splashed in typical otter fashion. That winter the shipwrecked crew took eight hundred of them.

To the fur-conscious Russians, however, the coats of these strange animals must have aroused even more admiration than the flesh. The velvety fur was so soft and luxurious that a man's hand almost drifted out of sight in it. It was the finest fur they had ever seen. The eight hundred pelts were carefully preserved.

On December 8, Bering died of scurvy on the lonely island which bears his name. Several other members of the crew also died. But with the coming of spring the shipwrecked sailors began salvaging materials to build a boat that might take them home. Led by Bering's first lieutenant, Sven Waxell, and a widely known and heavy-drinking German naturalist who had accompanied the party, Georg Wilhelm Steller, the survivors returned to Russia with the eight hundred otter pelts.

Soon the furs were being displayed in St. Petersburg. Imaginations were fired and shortly the *promyshlenniki,* the tough and resourceful Russian free-lance fur traders, were headed for the islands Bering had discovered. The sea otter, which for centuries had drifted idly on his back in the tide, was suddenly under attack. His coat became the most valuable fur of all times.

The Russians hired or forced the native Aleuts to help them capture the animals. Men in boats surrounded the otters. With clubs, stones, guns and spears they kept the animals diving until they were exhausted, then killed them and dragged them into their boats.

If a howling storm should catch a group of sea otters out on the rocks, the natives would slip up on them unheard in the dark and dispatch them quickly. Even nets were used to ensnare them in the water where they swam.

While the natives themselves, now victims of violence and new diseases, captured otters, ships shuttled furs back to Russia in a brisk trade that could not last. Gradually the Russians realized they were cutting into the seed stock. After a hundred years of exploitation the animals were becoming increasingly scarce.

By the time the United States bought Alaska and its islands from the Russians for $7,200,000 in 1867, the sea-otter business was only a shadow of what it had been in earlier times. This, however, did not keep American crews from going after the hard-pressed sea otters that remained. Prime pelts were bringing $250 or more.

The sea otter had once occupied the Pacific Coast all the way from the islands of Japan to Lower California. By 1900 they had been so heavily hunted over all this range that they still held out only in the wildest and most remote corners of the Aleutians. In 1910 only thirty-four pelts were recorded for North America, and the federal government closed the hunting season. The following year Great Britain, Japan and the United States signed a treaty which brought international protection to the sea otter. Some said it was already too late.

Two years later, on March 3, 1913, the federal government established the Aleutian Islands Wildlife Reservation to protect and manage native birds, reindeer, fur-bearing animals and fish. Today, with 2,720,235 acres, the Aleutian Islands National Wildlife Refuge is one of the biggest areas in the federal refuge system. It includes all but six of the major islands in the Aleutians.

This refuge holds the world's greatest nesting colonies of sea birds. Birds nest on the volcanic ledges, on sand beaches and in the hills. There are crested auklets, tufted puffins, horned puffins, kittiwakes, fulmars, red-throated loons, red-faced cormorants, ptarmigan, swans, emperor geese and snow buntings, a total, in fact, of 140 bird species in the refuge.

Unimak Island, at the eastern end of the refuge, has populations of caribou and the Alaska brown bear. Portions of the refuge are open to hunting of upland game, migratory birds and big game. Up to twenty-five permits a year are issued for hunting the brown bear. All the waters around the islands are open to sport fishing. There is good fishing for silver salmon, in some places as late as October. Dolly Varden is another fish taken on the refuge as long in the season as anglers can stand the weather. Visitors, however, are uncommon on most of the Aleutian Islands.

Early in the 1930s reports began filtering out of Alaska that sea otters were being sighted occasionally along the chain. Then in 1936 a government expedition discovered a small but flourishing colony of them living in the kelp beds around Amchitka Island. This halted all arguments about whether or not the sea otter had become extinct. Given protection, they had gradually built up their numbers.

Amchitka, long, narrow and hilly, is out toward the western end of the chain. It is thirty-five miles long and three to five miles wide. Around it are hazardous reefs, and it offers only one very poor harbor, facts that doubtless discouraged the fur traders and perhaps saved the otter.

Most of the time food supplies were no pressing problem for the sea otters. They had constant supplies from the ocean. If killer whales took a few of their numbers, the otters seemed well able to withstand these inroads. What they had needed most was protection from man.

In 1938 a flourishing pod of ninety-four sea otters was discovered near Monterey, California. Today several hundred live between there and San Miguel Island. Meanwhile the otters have spread from Amchitka to surrounding islands.

Will this marine mammal spread along the Pacific Coast until he has repopulated all his ancestral territory? Most biologists think not. Karl W. Kenyon, a Fish and Wildlife Service research biologist who studied sea otters extensively, said, "I believe that polluted waters will prevent their survival close to large centers of human population. The difficulty lies in the extremely soft and delicate fur which is protected only to a minor degree by its few, scattered guard hairs. If even a small amount of oil floating on the water surface coats the fur fibers, the insulating properties are lost. Soiled and wet animals, unprotected from the cold sea water, soon chill and die." A full half century after being given full protection, the sea otter had spread back to less than one fifth of the coast line he originally occupied.

An adult sea otter is about four feet long, and may

weigh eighty pounds. Unlike the seals with their flippers, the otter has small front feet. His hind feet are webbed, which helps mightily in his underwater maneuvering.

He flourishes on a sea-food diet. Sea urchins, in some places so abundant you can look down from a rowboat and see a green carpet of them covering the ocean floor, are often the otter's main dish. He also eats mussels and snails. An adult sea otter must eat a fourth of his body weight in sea foods every day.

While the sea otter eats, he drifts on his back and uses his chest for a table. Animals that feed on mollusks are frequently hard pressed for ways to open these bivalves to extract the food inside. The gull that has learned to break open clams by dropping them from on high might take a lesson from the sea otter floating on the waves. The otter has learned to use tools.

This practical habit was observed by Olaus J. Murie, who surveyed the animal life of the Aleutians while working with the federal government in 1936 and 1937. He described how the otters break clams against flat rocks held on their chests. They grasp the mollusk in their front feet and bang it against the rock until it cracks. More recent observers have classified this as an infrequent act which is apparently more common along the California coast than in Aleutian waters.

"When feeding," wrote Murie, "the sea otter has a habit of rolling over occasionally in a complete turn, then continuing with its repast. Sometimes it performs this roll with a rock and mollusk both on the chest. Naturally, it must clasp both of these objects to its body during the roll, but it does this very adroitly and casually, and it continues unconcerned with its meal."

How or why the sea otter learned to use rocks as tools is open to speculation. The teeth of the otter have developed into efficient crushing devices with which he can crack many of the hard-shelled foods he collects. Investigators report that old otters' teeth are often cavity-ridden. One might even speculate that it was a sea otter with a toothache that first decided to be a Stone Age animal.

So fond of resting on his back is the sea otter that he even sleeps this way, sometimes using a paw to shade his eyes. Why doesn't he drift away on the tides? Because he is anchored. He often rests with a ribbon of kelp across his middle.

Gulls probably cause him as much trouble as anything. They whirl around in screaming flocks to catch the scraps from his table or to rob him if the chance presents itself. The otter, like a mischievous boy in a swimming pool, will sometimes splash water in a gull's face.

For mothers everywhere the female sea otter stands as a model. Her pup is almost always within reach. As she drifts on her back, she has the pup curled up for a nap on her chest. When she dives she may leave him floating like a cork, and on occasion the bald eagle may pick him up. But she will more likely grasp him under one arm and take him along, sometimes patting him first as if to tell him that he is about to get a dunking. Late studies indicate that the female sea otter has only one young every two years.

Gradually their numbers are growing. Today wildlife authorities believe there may be twenty-five thousand sea otters. Scattered as they are and given full protection, they are no longer in serious danger of disappearing. The story of how the sea otter was saved is only one of the unusual animal stories from this great wildlife refuge. Another one which wildlife managers are unraveling is the Aleutian Islands version of that fabled conflict between the fox and the goose.

In the 1800s with the sea otter disappearing, Alaskan fur traders were looking for new sources of income. They turned to the blue fox, which is a dark phase of the arctic fox. Biologists now know that across the Aleutian chain it was only on Attu that blue foxes were native when Bering came along. In succeeding years every island that could be conveniently reached was supplied with blue-fox breeding stock. Only four minor islands were missed. The Aleutian Islands became a sprawling fur farm with foxes feeding on the wildlife. All the fur collectors had to do was come back every few years and take the foxes.

In 1936, when he went to the Aleutians to study wildlife there, Olaus Murie was especially interested in what the foxes were eating. He had no difficulty finding them; they were everywhere.

At that time there were no longer any Canada geese nesting on the long, narrow Amchitka Island out near the west end of the archipelago. Seven foxes had been released there in 1921. The natives insisted that before the foxes came to Amchitka, geese had nested there in abundance.

The Aleutian Canada goose is a small subspecies not found in any other part of the world. In addition to its small size, which is usually four and a half to five and a half pounds, it has a high-pitched "luk-luk-luk" call instead of the honk typical of the Canada goose. It is marked much like any of the several other subspecies of Canada geese except for a white collar at the base of the stocking on its neck.

The Aleutian Canada goose once nested abundantly throughout much of the archipelago all the way out to Attu. But after his studies in 1936, Murie said ". . . they had disappeared in most of the islands, and our total observations indicated that only a few pairs remained in the Aleutians." He placed the blame on the blue foxes, and in addition thought that hunting might be making dangerous inroads in the brood stock along the flyways to the south. As it later turned out, hunting probably deserves little, if any, blame in the decimation of these geese.

One man who dreamed for years of bringing these little geese back to their ancestral islands was Robert D. Jones, Jr., manager of the Aleutian Islands National Wildlife Refuge. Few people have ever come to understand the wildlife populations of these islands better than Jones. During World War II he spent forty-two months of military duty on several of the islands, including Amchitka. Unlike most of his companions, Jones thoroughly enjoyed his tour in the Aleutians. He became completely fascinated with the string of islands, their wildlife, history and remote wilderness character. He spent his spare time hiking across the islands and climbing the peaks. Before the war he had completed his studies in biology at South Dakota State College. After the war he stayed in the Aleutians and in 1948 became the first manager of the eleven-hundred-mile-long refuge. One of the projects Jones and other refuge people were already contemplating was working out a method of re-establishing geese on their ancestral islands.

But before the wildlife people could bring the geese back to any of these islands it seemed obvious that something had to be done about the foxes. To Bob Jones, this meant only one thing—eliminate the foxes, wipe them out.

"This, as any biologist recognizes, is a difficult task. Several of the wildlife experts gathering in Anchorage to discuss the project felt, in fact, that the best they could hope for would be to "control" the foxes, which meant simply to hold down their numbers. Jones held out. "Without complete success," he argued, "only failure can result."

The first island chosen for the goose project was Amchitka, where Jones knew every fog-bound hill and stream. In 1950 Jones and his staff hid strychnine pellets in one thousand one-inch cubes of harbor-seal blubber. Then he hiked around Amchitka and planted the pellets on beaches, especially around Constantine Harbor and Kirilof Point, where he had seen fresh fox tracks. Here he also saw the tracks of innumerable house cats and stray dogs, descendants of soldiers' abandoned pets.

He went back the following year with a large supply of poison which he spread on the beach.

Later, when he hiked around Amchitka several times, he could find only one set of fox tracks on the island, the lone survivor of a once-flourishing population of animals that Nature had not put there.

The refuge staff now faced the challenge of locating the remaining breeding colony of the Aleutian Canada geese. These, according to the plan, might eventually supply captive birds to raise for restocking the islands. Am-

chitka, free now of its foxes, would be the first to get its
geese back.

To begin with, the wildlife men knew that only four
minor islands had escaped being stocked with foxes during the 1920s when fur prices were high. One of these had
to be the place where the geese might still be nesting. The
best candidate was Buldir Island, most remote of all the
islands in the Aleutians.

Travel is a major problem in a refuge composed of
eleven hundred miles of islands. In the Aleutians, refuge
workers travel in many ways. Commercial airlines haul
them to Adak, two thirds of the way across the chain. This
is the jumping-off point for operations in the western section of the refuge. From there they travel often by cour-
tesy of the Coast Guard or the Navy. But the most important travel vehicles they have is a fleet of three Grand
Banks dories, built in Massachusetts and modified in Alaska
for use with outboard engines. The dories are docked at
strategic spots along the refuge. There are years when the
refuge manager travels two thousand miles in these boats.

At times the seas are so high that to take even the dory
to the edge of an island would risk destruction on the
rocks. On such occasions, when they have wanted badly
enough to go ashore, as they did once to check the foxes
on the little island of Kasatochi, Jones and his assistant
are likely to anchor their dory two hundred yards offshore
and swim to the island in "wet suit" diving equipment.

Buldir, about four miles long by two and a half wide, is
a rugged, mountainous dome-shaped island rising more
than two thousand feet above the sea. There is a single
small beach at the mouth of a little valley near Northwest
Point, the only suitable place on the entire island for taking a boat to shore. Elsewhere the shores are marked by
cliffs rising directly from the water's edge or separated
from the sea by narrow rock and sand beaches.

Along the beach and valley floor rye grass and wild
celery grow three feet high, and so dense a man has
trouble pushing his way through. Fog and drizzle keep

the vegetation heavy with moisture most of the time. Farther up the slopes, beyond the rye grass, is typical arctic tundra where heather and dwarf willows hug the ground.

On June 25, 1962, Jones and his assistant, Vernon D. Berns, a wildlife-management graduate of Colorado State University, returned to Buldir. Along with their dory *Dipper*, they were lowered from the deck of a cooperating Coast Guard cutter. Almost at once they were caught in the day-and-night bedlam made by millions of screaming gulls and other sea birds which literally filled the air. Added to this was the roaring and grunting of ten thousand sea lions living there on the rocks under refuge protection. The only signs that man had ever been there before were a few disintegrating buildings, remnants of the Great War, and an aging P-38 wrecked on a hillside. This time, in what Jones considers the most thrilling moment in all his refuge work, they saw four Aleutian Canada geese flush from heavy cover, and shortly heard their goslings cheeping.

The following July, Jones led a six-man team back, prepared to stay a week on Buldir. They spent the first four days huddled in their tents, bombarded constantly by high winds and driving rains. When the weather broke, they hiked up to Kittywake Pond, counted more than a hundred adult geese and found five goslings on the lake. The startled gray goslings ran up a slope and the refuge workers scrambled behind them, caught them and gently put them into cardboard cartons which they carried on back packs.

They explored other parts of the island and estimated the total goose population there at 250 to 300 adults, probably all the remaining Aleutian Canada geese in the world. By the end of the week they had captured eighteen goslings which they installed in a nine-foot by nine-foot nylon tent heated by a flameless heater. They fed the goslings a mixture of chick starter, egg yolks and finely chopped sedges and grasses.

They packed the young birds two to a box and put them aboard the plane for Anchorage, where they were flown to Denver, Colorado.

Meanwhile the Fish and Wildlife Service was taking the first steps toward a program designed to help save rare and endangered species of birds. They had hired career wildlife worker C. Eugene Knoder from Ohio to set up the program temporarily on the Monte Vista National Wildlife Refuge in the high desert country of south-central Colorado. Sixteen of the Aleutian Canada geese reached Knoder safely. As they matured, Knoder, whose favorite family pet back in Columbus, Ohio, had been a Canada goose in a neighborhood of French poodles, determined that ten of them were females and six were ganders.

Here then was brood stock for a wild goose once given up as lost by many competent biologists. It may, however, prove unnecessary to bring captive goslings back to the Aleutians. The foxes are gone from Amchitka and other islands are also being cleared. The best evidence indicates that hunting does not get the blame for reducing the goose flock. Following the location of this fine population of geese, Fish and Wildlife Service biologist and specialist in Aleutian Island wildlife Karl W. Kenyon said, "Hunting would have caused a general depletion of the population. Where foxes were introduced," he added, "the goose is completely gone. On Buldir, where foxes were not introduced, the population is prosperous." The Buldir geese, obviously a healthy lot, may spread out and return to Amchitka by themselves, and to other islands as well, as foxes are removed.

If not, there are always the captive birds for seed stock.

No matter which method ultimately brings the geese back, the staff on the Aleutian Islands National Wildlife Refuge has the satisfaction of knowing that these birds can nest again and raise their young on islands where they nested before Vitus Bering left the shores of Siberia that day in 1741.

Agassiz
Where the Ducks Came Back

Agassiz National Wildlife Refuge

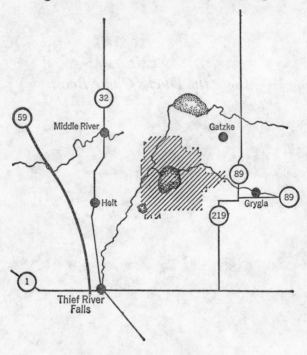

MINNESOTA

6

I turned from the highway half a mile north of Holt, Minnesota, and drove eleven miles out across the flat country to a cluster of squat, white buildings dwarfed by a hundred-foot fire tower. Out of the shadows to announce me came an ancient golden retriever who thought he was a watchdog. But refuge manager Herb Dill was off on an errand, so while I waited I climbed the tower for a look at this famous refuge.

Here in the flat marshes and pothole country hundreds of thousands of southbound mallards, teal, scaup and other waterfowl stop to feed and rest in a land of abundance. A few decades ago people around Holt might have argued with logic on their side that never again would this region appeal to large numbers of ducks and geese.

In those days the waterfowl would look down on this countryside and fly on. Once it had been a haven for their ancestors. But if they felt any faint instinctive twinge of attraction to it, the dry, dusty and sometimes smoking earth below promised no rest or food.

Now, however, I could see mile on mile of marshes and bogs dotted with thickets and laced with waterways. A marsh hawk cruised at low altitudes across the wetlands. Mallards passed back and forth as they must have a century ago, and to the east a small flock of Canada geese settled in on one of the diked reservoirs. This refuge is one of the best examples anywhere of how man can, if he chooses, untangle his earlier mistakes and bring waterfowl back to a region where history had them in the first place. This famed waterfowl area is one of the most northern of the refuges in the Mississippi Flyway. Originally it was called Mud Lake National Wildlife Refuge. This name was changed some years ago to Agassiz National Wildlife Refuge, partly because it lies in a bay of the ancient bed of the pre-glacial Lake Agassiz. The refuge covers 60,744 acres. On its south and east are two Minnesota Conservation Department wildlife-management areas, the Elm Lake and Eckvoll areas totaling 21,600 acres, altogether 82,344 acres of wildlife habitat.

Herb Dill told me much of the history of dashed hopes and fruitless labors buried in the past of this refuge area. "The first settlers came into the area," he said, "in the 1890s to claim homesteads." Even then it was a region more suited to wildlife than to agriculture. To the west, south and east were thirty-eight thousand acres of grasslands. There was a thirteen-thousand-acre swamp where great spruce and tamarack were interspersed with white birch and aspen. The sphagnum moss of the forest floor was a huge sponge, perpetually saturated. And there were broad shallow lakes, including Mud Lake, for which the refuge was first named.

There was no early land rush. The growing season was short, the winters long and cold. And water covered much of the land. "By 1910," Dill said, "there were no more than thirty homesteads on this area. Most of the early settlers were bachelors who proved their claims, then sold their land and moved out."

They kept some livestock and harvested the wild hay but mostly they lived off the products of the marshes. They could shoot rabbits, ducks, moose and grouse as they needed them, and when they couldn't eke out a living from farming, they could trap for furs and hunt game for the cash market.

The marsh grew thick with luxuriant stands of cattails,

bulrushes, phragmites, big burweed, spikerush and white-top. And in the ponds were coontail, pondweeds, duck-weed and water milfoil. Mink, muskrat and moose prospered and waterfowl came by the hundreds of thousands. "Shore birds were here in huge flocks in the sloughs and potholes," said Dill, "and sharp-tailed grouse and prairie chickens were very common."

Then in 1909 eighteen townships in the eastern part of Marshall County were organized into Judicial Drainage District No. 11. Marshall County was determined to see the great marsh in its eastern section drained. The enthusiastic citizens floated a bond issue to raise $475,000 and pay for the drainage work. In Holt, 1910 was a boom year. By 1914, two hundred homesteaders were in the area.

Part of this new drainage district lay in the 4500-acre, shallow and marshy Mud Lake. Here was a great natural storage reservoir that held water back in wet years and rationed it out in periods of drought. Consequently the Thief River running along the west side of the refuge and fed by the marshes was almost never dry. And in the peat bogs around Mud Lake it was hard to tell where soil stopped and water began. The "uplands" were scarcely twenty feet above the lowest levels. For wildlife this was a wonderfully wet and productive world.

Then came the steel monsters to cut arteries back into the heart of the marsh and let the water drain away. All this was to be paid for by a drainage tax which the farmers, blessed now with fertile dry land, could pay from their profits. In this manner, the promoters claimed, the district could retire its bonded indebtedness. But it never worked out that way. Marshall County farmers could not find the money to pay their drainage taxes.

Finally, when Marshall County was hopelessly in debt, the state had to step in and set up an aid fund to enable the county to meet its obligations. The drainage project, instead of bringing its promised riches, had turned the county into a disaster area.

"Approximately 250 miles of ditches were dug in what is now the refuge," said Herb Dill. "With the drying up of Mud Lake, and the general lowering of the water table here, fires began to break out. It took some of the peat soils four years to dry out completely and as they dried, fires became worse. Some of the peat beds burned for years and left mineral soils and hardpan exposed."

In 1914–15 fires were burning fourteen inches deep, destroying humus and burning down haystacks as they came to them. By this time the Thief River had ceased to flow except in the wettest months. In 1933 the last of the really big fires burned over most of the spruce-tamarack bogs that had for countless centuries been too wet to burn.

"The uncertainties of farming," Dill said, "finally forced all but fifty or sixty homesteaders to move out. Those that stayed lived by haying, grazing abandoned farmlands, and not paying taxes." With the water gone, waterfowl and shore birds had quickly disappeared. Only the sharp-tailed grouse benefited from the farming.

"Fires," said Dill, "and the lowering of the water table let the aspen groves spread out until they replaced several thousand acres of spruce and tamarack. Willow brush claimed large acreages. Natural grasslands were replaced by quackgrass and weeds which added to the fire hazard during dry periods."

Robbed now of their moisture, the peat soils began to settle. Some bridges, built at ground level, stood six feet above their approaches.

In the mid-thirties the federal government, through the Resettlement Administration, bought 61,744 acres of the drained lands, for which it paid Minnesota $368,500. What has happened since to the area can be seen in striking contrast in the half a million acres lying to the east of the refuge. These lands outside the refuge look almost as they did in 1937.

But inside the refuge, wildlife managers, hastening to undo the work of the drainage district, designed systems of dikes to retain the water. The reclamation work continued right up to World War II. And even today it has not all been restored. But, as Herb Dill explained to me, "Twenty-four thousand acres of marsh have been reclaimed. There are thirteen pools ranging in size from 150 to 12,000 acres. We have sixty miles of roads and forty-eight miles of dikes. And we have structures to control water levels on all our marshes."

What has this done for wildlife? In Agassiz National Wildlife Refuge, ducks have come back to raise their young. Fifteen species now nest on these restored marshes each summer and produce as many as thirty thousand ducklings a year, more than any other refuge in the Mississippi Flyway. Most common are the mallards, blue-winged teal, and gadwalls. There are wood ducks, American widgeons, canvasbacks, pintails, redheads and shovelers along with ringneck ducks, lesser scaups and ruddies.

And at the peak of fall migration the local ducks may have a quarter of a million southbound ducks and geese drop in among them to feed and rest. "As a duck producer," the late J. Clark Salyer II once told me, "Agassiz, acre for acre, ranks with the best Canada has to offer."

For neighbors, the waterfowl have thriving populations of grouse, moose, black bear, and whitetail deer.

How does a refuge manager keep track of all these boarders? Migrating ducks are censused in the fall from small planes by observers who have developed uncanny accuracy in estimating the numbers of ducks in flocks of all sizes.

To learn how many ducklings a refuge is producing, there is an early spring count to find out how many pairs have established nesting territories. This is checked both from the ground and the air and the figures are compared with those of previous years. Then the refuge staff, once a week, drives over a thirty-seven-mile route to count the broods of ducks to learn how production compares with previous years.

But to trace the travels of waterfowl along their flyways the biologists must catch them in large numbers and band or otherwise mark them. Herb Dill decided in 1948 to speed up the chore of trapping waterfowl. He invented the equipment now used in many parts of the world. He was then manager of the Swan Lake National Wildlife Refuge near Sumner, Missouri. The usual waterfowl trap at the time was an affair concocted of sagging chicken wire with a funnel-shaped approach into which ducks were baited. If things went especially well a morning's work might see two hundred ducks caught, banded and released. The wary Canada goose, however, was not nearly so easily fooled.

Dill, and his co-worker Howard Thornsberry, conceived the idea of throwing a net over concentrations of feeding waterfowl. There was but one way to get a net out over the birds before they had time to lift off: shoot it out with an explosive. Dill and Thornsberry fashioned a simple cannon out of steel tubing, folded the net carefully, tied its leading edge to projectiles which would fit down into the cannon. "We started out," said Dill, "using dynamite, and blew up a few things at first."

Over the years they found better explosives for the task, and perfected their equipment and techniques until they were making catches of two and three hundred ducks or geese in a single shot. They used three cannons to propel the net.

Shortly their cannon net was in use all over the world on a wide variety of birds. It became a common wildlife-management tool wherever men needed to catch large numbers of birds in a hurry and without harming them.

Canada geese, which for many years no longer nested in the area at all, now build a hundred or more nests a year on this refuge, and produce three to four hundred goslings. There is room for more. Predators have been a problem in bringing geese back to Agassiz. When I last visited this refuge the manager showed me their latest design for a goose-nest platform. They had tried floating platforms but raccoons climbed onto them. They had built log cribs but muskrats tunneled beneath them and the nests washed away.

Then they began spending winter days welding steel towers seven feet high. The top is covered with woven wire. Set out in four feet of water, these frames hold the nest three feet above the surface and predators must climb a steel pole to reach it. They are slid out onto the ice, and when the ice goes out in the spring the nesting structures settle into place.

And the big-game animals on Agassiz have prospered along with the waterfowl. By 1937 the moose population had dwindled to three lonely-looking beasts occasionally spotted by local people. Today 130 moose live on the refuge. "This is about one and a half per section," Dill told me, "and that's a lot of moose. Once or twice a year we'll get a call from a farmer who is having trouble with a moose that has wandered off the refuge. They don't go over fences like deer; they go through them the same way they crash through an aspen thicket. They just stick their heads out level and push everything aside. You can't drive a moose back onto the refuge," says Dill, "in fact, you can't drive a moose anywhere."

No one can say what the population of whitetail deer was on the area when the refuge was established, but now it is one of the finest herds in all of Minnesota. Hundreds of deer hunters come to the refuge for the annual managed hunt held in cooperation with the Minnesota Department of Conservation. There are usually twelve hundred deer here prior to the fall hunt.

The refuge people want the deer population reduced each year to six or eight per square mile, the safe winter carrying capacity of the refuge habitat. This generally means that hunters take home about 320 deer in the average season. These are likely to be the largest deer taken in Minnesota. Many weigh two hundred pounds hog dressed, and three-hundred-pounders are not rare.

Some forty thousand people a year visit this wildlife refuge. Most are content to drive along the secondary road that stretches across the southern edge of the area, past Green Stump Pool, South Pool and refuge headquarters.

Some stop and climb the fire tower. Bird watchers have listed 225 species of birds on this refuge. Occasionally visitors even see a moose. Or in autumn they may spot a black bear fattening on blueberries and wild plums. Public use of this area, however, must be limited; people and nesting ducks do not mix. When the deer hunters are there, the ducks have already gone south.

This is a refuge where wildlife has a bright future. In spite of the work already done, there are still large parts of the area that can be diked and flooded to grow still more wild crops for waterfowl. And as water comes back to this corner of the ancient bed of the glacial Lake Agassiz, the ducks and the geese should continue to build their numbers and prove the wisdom of whatever force in the scheme of things first designated this as wetlands.

For Brant and Bird Watchers

Brigantine National Wildlife Refuge

7

Every wild creature has his place in the order of the universe. Some live on the mountain slopes, some in the deserts and others in the swamps. For the American brant, *Branta bernicla hrota,* home is by the edge of the sea. These little sea geese nest in the arctic just beyond reach of the tide; they migrate over the ocean and spend the winter in the tidal basins along the Atlantic Coast.

When November brings the hint of winter to the shores of New Jersey, the brant come in during the night. The next morning the manager of the Brigantine National Wildlife Refuge will see them, buoyant but sedate, on the open bay or across the dikes in the big shallow pools. They ride the water in tight formation, their black vests turned toward him. There are perhaps 150 of them.

This, however, is only the vanguard. Somewhere up the coast most of the brant still wing their way southward. The following day the refuge manager may find, not 150 brant, but fifty thousand of them, because this is the precipitous fashion in which they return each autumn to their wintering grounds. Within two days' time brant are everywhere, sitting on the water and passing back and forth in long wavering lines across the bays.

The waterfowl hunter rejoices and the bird watcher happily records the event on his check list. The refuge manager watches closely to detect any changing trends in their populations.

There is little that is spectacular about a brant. This is one of the smallest of all our wild geese, scarcely larger than a big drake mallard. He has a short stout neck and a small head. His breast, neck, head and even his short beak are black, except for an irregular patch of white on the sides of his neck. While his back is brownish, his sides are light colored with darker bars, and the sides of his rump are white. He rides high on the water, is graceful in his movements, and when he feeds he tips up like a puddle duck with his tail pointed skyward.

They all spend the winter along a short stretch of the Atlantic Coast from New Jersey to North Carolina. At least 40 percent of them spend some part of their lives on Brigantine, the most important single area in their wintering territory.

This refuge covers 13,442 acres of salt marsh and sand hills scarcely sixty miles from Philadelphia and 112 miles from the Manhattan skyline. The Intracoastal Waterway passes through the refuge, the "New York Road" is only a mile to the west, and six miles away is the traffic-laden Garden State Parkway. At night the lights of nearby Atlantic City are plainly visible from the refuge. The wonder of it is that, in the midst of such concentrations of homes and cities, we have held out fragments of land for wildlife.

You will find these refuges along the coast, scattered in a great chain of wildlife safety zones from Maine to Miami. There are such names as Moosehorn, Parker River, Great Meadows, Monomy, Troy Meadows, Killcochook and Cape Romain. Brigantine was established near the middle of the chain in 1939. These Atlantic Coast refuges are about two hundred miles apart, which enables migrating ducks and geese to find ice-free resting and feeding areas a jump ahead of advancing winter storms.

Bird watchers in great numbers migrate to Brigantine from such human nesting areas as Philadelphia, New York and Washington. There are at least three reasons why this is one of the country's most popular bird-watching areas.

It is, first of all, close to several million people. With both fresh and saltwater habitat, it has a great variety of birds. And bird watching here is easy. Visitors drive along the tops of the dikes studying birds from the comfort of the family car. And best of all, the birds are undisturbed.

Some years sixty thousand bird watchers come to Brigantine. If the refuge manager asks Washington for ten thousand copies of the Brigantine bird list (which includes nearly three hundred species), they are sent without a lifted eyebrow. "Another refuge," said one worker in Washington, "may have obtained one thousand copies of its bird list several years ago and still have half of them left." Bird-club members come by the bus load. Some years ago the National Audubon Society visited Brigantine as part of its annual meeting, and many people from foreign lands have visited here, including the president of the National Audubon Society of Japan.

The avocet, a large and impressive shore bird with an upturned beak, was considered extremely rare anywhere east of the Mississippi. A few years ago, however, word came that one had arrived at Brigantine National Wildlife Refuge. Excited bird watchers called the refuge manager from many parts of the East, then began arriving from as far away as Ohio and Michigan. Since then, avocets have been seen even more frequently at Brigantine, sometimes several at once.

On an autumn day I drove over the dikes of this refuge, and waterfowl dominated the scene. Black ducks bounded into the air from the bulrushes as we passed; little ruddy ducks and teal swam around the millet that grows in the fresh-water pools. American bitterns, camouflaging themselves against the brown vegetation, stood motionless, their long yellow beaks pointing skyward as we passed.

A flock of two hundred greater snow geese had just arrived from their breeding grounds in the arctic, probably en route to the Pea Island National Wildlife Refuge on the coast of North Carolina. And there were Canada geese —some now nest on this refuge and they have been stopping in growing numbers during fall and winter months.

A laughing gull in his immature grayish plumage flew along the dike until well past all other gulls, then dropped a clam he carried in his beak. His elevation was perhaps forty feet and he peeled off rapidly and followed the mollusk to the ground. He picked it up again, carried it aloft and dropped it repeatedly until it broke and he had clam on the halfshell.

But brant dominated the Brigantine scene. We estimated that eighty thousand of them occupied the refuge at the time. Almost everywhere we looked, wavering lines of brant shifted like smoke against the horizon. Others came in near us to land on the fresh-water pools behind the barrier dikes. Brant file no flight plan. Unlike Canada geese they have never adopted those impressive V formations. Instead they simply bound into the air and fly away in a group; positions shift as they fly. Their pace is slow and when on local flights they travel at low elevations.

How many brant will come back to winter along the coast each year? No one can yet predict this. This goose nests in the cold, barren reaches of the arctic, where in a few brief weeks each summer they produce their young. For years this phase of the brant's life was a mystery. Then in the summer of 1953 a Canadian biologist, Thomas W. Barry, traveled beyond the Arctic Circle to live with the Eskimos and learn more about the brant's secrets. Barry, working for his master's degree at Cornell University, had the financial support of several conservation and research organizations. He arrived at the Boas River on the coast of Southampton Island in the Northwest Territories ahead of the birds.

The brant, he learned, arrived each year in force on the 7th and 8th of June. Their schedule is a tight one and they live at the mercy of the weather. If they are to bring off a family of young, there is scant time for dawdling. If spring melts the snows on schedule, nearly all the nesting brant begin incubation within a ten-day period.

But spring may come late to the arctic, and the frustrated brant then fly restlessly over the tundra. Barry concluded that they have already mated before they arrive, and each day their nesting is delayed may cut down the number of eggs they lay.

Late-nesting brant also risk having their young trapped in the arctic by an early winter. In the spring of 1957 Barry discovered a group of twenty-one young brant frozen in the ice where the first winter storm caught them the previous year. "They were well preserved," he reported in the *Journal of Wildlife Management,* "and nothing could be found wrong with them except that their feather development was four to five days short of allowing them to fly."

The brant's domain on this arctic scene is a narrow strip of seashore covered with a sedge known as "brant grass," which supplies most of their summer food.

In three summers' work with the nesting brant, Barry, aided by the Eskimos, banded enough adults to uncover still more of their secrets. He learned that they return to the same nesting area year after year. They begin to nest when two or three years old and continue for perhaps five seasons. Some seasons he found at least 60 percent of the adults not nesting. Fortunately, the future of the bird is not dependent on any single summer's production. Losses forced on them by weather one year may be recouped the next, and if not then, perhaps the year after.

By late August or early September they are headed southward with whatever young they manage to raise. And by early November they have returned to the Atlantic Coast.

This little sea goose has, for ages, been a cherished part of the autumn scene for east coast waterfowlers. Those who await them in blinds and boxes along the salt marshes have developed special techniques for hunting them. For the true brant fancier the whole year points toward November. In former years, before the laws changed, April was important too, because the brant could be hunted on their northward migration.

One man who looked forward to brant shooting was ornithologist Arthur Cleveland Bent. He described it in one of his famous volumes dealing with the life histories of American birds. "On Monomoy," he said, "our brant shooting is done from boxes located on favorable points on sand bars near the feeding grounds. The box is well made and watertight, six feet long, by four feet wide, and four feet deep; big enough for three men; it is sunken into the sand deep enough to be covered at high tide. . . ."

That was an age of techniques now long illegal. Not only did hunters engage in spring shooting, but near their box blinds they also tethered live decoys on the sand. "The brant feed at low tide away off on the eelgrass beds," Bent added, "but as the rising tide covers the grass too deeply, they are driven to seek other feeding grounds or sanding places, and in flying about will often come to the decoys."

Brant have long held the reputation of being one of the finest of waterfowl when properly served. Bent said, "I can not think of any more delicious bird than a fat young brant, roasted just right and served hot, with a bottle of good Burgundy." Then sadly he added, "Both the bird and the bottle are now hard to get; alas, the good old days have passed."

However, forty years later, the brant is still one of the most popular waterfowl hunted along the New Jersey coast. The modern brant hunter equips himself with a sneak box and a flat-bottomed gunning scow into which he piles at least a dozen and a half life-like decoys. If he is a confirmed brant hunter, and a man of imagination, he may even build a special dog compartment into his boat for his retriever, then add gun racks, padded lounging chair and shelves for shells and his coffee thermos.

Having chosen a spot where the birds will trade back and forth to feed at low tide, he pulls his boat up in the marsh and camouflages it with marsh grass and seaweed. The decoys are slightly downwind and not too far out. Now it is a matter of waiting. Chances are there will be roast brant on the family table this night.

In 1939, when the Brigantine National Wildlife Refuge was established, the American brant numbered scarcely more than thirty thousand. Hunters and professional conservationists worried about their future. The brant, however, has since increased to two hundred thousand or more, depending on the year's nesting success. So, the late lamented "good old days" may not be as irretrievably lost as Bent feared, and at least some of the reason can be found in the wildlife management being practiced on Brigantine.

Brigantine was originally established on 2824 acres, which waterfowl biologists felt, even then, was not as much land as the brant and black ducks needed. Ten years later, in spite of a storm of protests from local hunters, the refuge was increased to 13,310 acres. "They thought," said the refuge manager, Henry Whitley, "this would close up all the marshes where they had hunted. I couldn't go to the barbershop, church or anywhere else without getting into an argument about the refuge." Local hunters have since learned that the refuge brought better, not worse, brant shooting. Today, around Oceanville or Atlantic City, few will argue against the refuge.

"Half a refuge manager's job," Whitley said, "is public relations." At no time of the year does this become more apparent than during the annual waterfowl season. In keeping with state and federal regulations, 21 percent of the Brigantine National Wildlife Refuge is opened annually to waterfowling. It is considered one of New Jersey's choice hunting areas. There are no drawings to determine who may hunt and no limits placed on numbers of hunters. The federal refuge workers join with state game agents to enforce laws during the hunting season.

Some say the flavor of the brant has changed drastically in recent years. And they may have a point, because some years ago the brant altered its eating habits to keep from starving to death.

Historic food of this bird is the ribbon-like eelgrass that, until some years ago, grew in great abundance in shallow tidal basins from Nova Scotia to North Carolina. Then about 1930 a blight mysteriously attacked the eelgrass all along the coast. With shocking suddenness the brant lost the major item in its winter diet. The birds turned then to bay cabbage, a marine algae. They have since prospered on the substitute. As they had done with eelgrass, the brant push bay cabbage ahead of them with their beaks and roll it up into balls, like a little pasta, before eating it.

Almost at once epicures along the coast noted that the once delicate flesh of the brant had become strong and unpleasant to the taste. Others still insist it's in the cooking. The brant meanwhile prospers on bay cabbage, little concerned that his change of eating habits distresses some of those who pursue him.

Over the years almost monumental efforts have been expended in behalf of the waterfowl in this refuge. Nailing up the sign of the flying goose was not enough. Henry Whitley, who began working on refuges during the early 1930s in his native Georgia, knew as did his boss, J. Clark Salyer II, in Washington, that the ducks especially needed more fresh-water areas on which to feed and rest. The brant could use the fresh-water areas for resting, and for escaping the occasional high seas that hit the bays. What they hoped to accomplish was to convert some of the salt-water marshes to fresh-water areas. This would enable them to grow duck-food plants such as millet and pond-weed.

"This meant building dikes," said Whitley, "then flushing the salt water out and letting fresh water in." They planned two large pools, one of nine hundred acres and another of seven hundred. The problem, however, was the soft muck bottom of the marsh. "In some places," Whitley said, "you could drive a piling down thirty-five or forty feet before it would fetch up."

Dikes had been built before on these marshes but always the fill had slipped out of sight or the dikes had cracked and the waves washed them into the bays. Whitley solved the problem. He knew from the history of the area that buried beneath the marsh was the bed of an old railroad that once ran from Philadelphia to Atlantic City. He used three miles of this sunken roadbed as the base for his first dike.

In 1952 trucks began hauling and dumping fill materials from the upland section of the refuge, and foot by foot the brown sand and rock inched out across the great marsh, cutting it into two sections with a dike six feet above high tide and wide enough on top for a two-lane road. Then other dikes were begun and within a few years the two great pools were complete with water valves. At low tide Whitley could now drain salt water out of the fields into the bay. Fresh water to refill the pools came from Lily Lake. "We had to flush them out three times," said Whitley, "to get rid of the salt water."

With fresh water in the pools, the refuge staff could draw down the water each spring and let the ground dry out. Each year wild millet, dropped there from the previous year's crop, reseeds itself. Shortly, the new crop is green on the fields and then the refuge manager begins to let water back into the pool and continues to increase its depth through the weeks as the wild millet grows. By autumn, when the ducks and geese come again, the millet has gone to seed and the waterfowl have food waiting. This is what Whitley's dikes did for Brigantine.

In autumn the fishing slacks off at Brigantine and later the waterfowl hunters are gone. Through the winter a few hardy bird watchers continue to come. The brant passing back and forth from bay to pool fatten on the bay cabbage, and eventually, when winter's harshest days are behind them, grow restless.

They leave Brigantine to the songbirds, gulls, a little flock of nesting Canada geese and a few gadwalls. The brant go back across their northward trails, retracing their flight to that strip of salt-washed brant grass along the

Arctic Ocean. And if the snows melt in good season, the old birds returning next autumn will bring with them large numbers of young to spend the winter scarcely a hundred miles from New York City.

Where Elk Come to Town

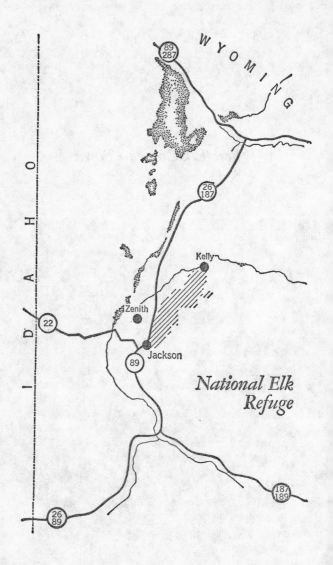

8

There is a time in autumn when the snows carry a message to the elk in the high country. Through the summer weeks they have wandered across the most remote mountain ranges, into the wildest valleys and along the edges of the alpine meadows. But now, with the coming of autumn, they are about to enter once more into one of the most unusual associations of man and wildlife since the beginning of civilization.

Down from the highest parts of Grand Teton National Park and the southern part of Yellowstone, elk begin moving along the trails ahead of the snowstorms. Most of them are headed down the valley of the Snake River toward the National Elk Refuge at Jackson, Wyoming. Here town people and one of the world's largest remaining herds of elk have wintered together for more than half a century.

Nowhere else in the country do so many big-game animals concentrate in plain view of so many people. School children, looking from classroom windows, see elk by the hundreds. Patients in the hospital on the eastern edge of town watch herds of elk while convalescing. Housewives pause in their dusting to see what the elk are doing at the back fence. And toddlers stand with faces glued to windows, watching the big animals wander over the open fields with the peaks of the Tetons forming a storybook backdrop. On a day in April each year the local Boy Scout

troops scour the refuge fields gathering antlers dropped by
the elk the month before. Eventually these are sold to
tourists and the Boy Scout troops collect the money.

Winter visitors come by the hundreds to Jackson Hole
to see the elk. In plain view of the highway that comes
south from Grand Teton National Park along the west
edge of the refuge are thousands of elk loafing or munch-
ing hay offered them by a concerned government. By going
first to refuge headquarters, which is in Jackson, elk watchers may even go out among the animals. Twice a day
during the coldest months refuge workers feed them hay
from large horse-drawn sleds. Years ago the refuge
manager began letting visitors ride these sleds and the
practice has never ended. In fact, through the years they
have added extra sleds on weekends to make room for
people. Thousands of elk crowd around the hay sleds while
ecstatic tourists run yards of film through all kinds of
cameras.

The people of Jackson, a bustling little resort town
nestled in the shadow of the magnificent Tetons, are proud
of their elk. They want it known far and wide that this
is "Elk Town." Over the gateway to the town square they
have stacked 5280 elk antlers in a great and grotesque
arch, which at Christmas time they decorate with colored
lights.

On one visit there I came by way of Yellowstone and
drove down to Jackson Hole from the north. It was late
September, an enchanted season in the Rockies. The
Tetons were like a picture postcard, filled with rugged
blue-gray peaks rising in sheer walls a mile and a half
above Jackson Lake, which was rimmed by dark-green
conifers. This is the season when the bugling of the elk is
at its height. There is something special about this wild,
high-pitched challenging call. Outdoorsmen have their
favorite wilderness sounds and the call of the bull elk belongs on the list. I never grow tired of hearing it again.

On this September evening, after we had eaten and settled before the open fireplace, refuge manager Larry

Means suddenly suggested, "Let's go out and listen to the elk bugle."

During the breeding season the bull elk, which may weigh eight hundred pounds and stand as high as a saddle horse, must be constantly ready to defend their harems. The mountains echo their bugling challenge. When two of these great animals meet in combat, there is a rattling of antlers accompanied by great shoving and grunting until one bull gives up. It's winner take all, and the cows seem unconcerned about the outcome.

We drove up through Mormon Row and out along Antelope Flats. Standing in the moonlight we shivered with the cold while assistant refuge manager Bill Blanchard put an elk call to his mouth. He produced a reedy note ending in a high-pitched whistle that should have fooled the elk for a mile around. But there was no answer.

At the next stop, however, we had better luck. Almost immediately there came an answering challenge from Blacktail Butte to the west. Then there was a bull bugling from the slopes to the east, and shortly not one but five bull elk were challenging each other back and forth across the valley. The coyotes, awakened now, set up their doleful yowling from every hill around us. The evening's music was fine and memorable, with elk and coyote alike in the best of voice. It was an experience all too rare in today's crowded world, but common enough around Jackson Hole.

Among the trappers and traders who first lived in the Rockies a "hole" was a level valley walled in by mountains. In 1829 trapper Bill Sublette named this valley for his partner Davey Jackson, because it was Jackson's favorite trapping ground. Then he named the largest lake in the valley Jackson Lake. Where did Jenny Lake, the second largest, get its name? Jenny was Jackson's Indian bride.

The valley stretches south from Yellowstone National Park for about fifty miles, and in many places it is twenty-five miles across. To the east is the Continental Divide and the Gros Ventre Range, to the west the Tetons. In the shadow of the Tetons the Snake River twists through the valley all the way from north to south.

Until 1889 there were no families living the year around in the valley. But that year the first of them came over the Teton Pass and, like the elk in autumn, followed the trails to the broad meadows of Jackson Hole. Now the great elk herd that had always traveled down through the hole to winter faced the most critical challenge in its long history.

Of all the deer on the continent the elk had once been the most widely distributed. But the herds in the East had disappeared early as hunters and settlers pushed westward. By the late 1800s the only sizable herds remaining were those that spent part of their lives in the highest and most inaccessible mountain ranges. The last of these big herds summered in the mountains of Yellowstone National Park and in the Tetons. Many of them also migrated down through Jackson Hole in the fall.

When the first settlers came these elk did not stop in autumn in Jackson Hole; they only passed through on their way south to the wild hay meadows of the Green River Valley, and the sagebrush flats of the Red Desert. But homesteaders brought livestock to eat the vegetation the elk had once wintered on. And they built fences across the valley. The elk, out of food and out of space, shortened their annual migration route; they began stopping for the winter around Jackson Hole.

Meanwhile the elk faced other threats. Meat hunters made steady inroads into the herd. Then sheep herders began, during the 1890s, to drive great flocks of sheep over the Teton Range from Idaho, to summer pasture in Jackson Hole. But the cattlemen, determined to keep the valley a land of cattle and game, ganged up in a great drive which, in 1896, forced the sheep, shepherds and all, back across the Tetons into Idaho. Oddest of all the elk's enemies were the tusk hunters who preyed upon the dwindling herds merely to extract their canine teeth. A pair of elk teeth sold for twenty-five dollars to members of the Elks Lodge, who proudly wore them as watch fobs and made necklaces of them for their ladies.

When the elk-tooth business really became big in 1904, Wyoming began sending in wardens to protect the animals, and the tooth robbers developed all manner of sly games to outwit their pursuers. The most famous of these gangs of poachers was headed by Bill Binkley and Charley Purdy. They frequently hunted in the half-million-acre game preserve which Wyoming had created in the Teton National Forest. They hid in dugouts and camouflaged their tracks by attaching elk hoofs to the bottom of their shoes or by walking with their snowshoes on backward.

Then one night in 1906 Tom Henshaw, near Kelly, was host to a mean-tempered posse of some thirty-five local ranchers who had seen more than enough of this elk-poaching business. They were determined to stop it, and after discussing the advisability of hanging Bill Binkley and Charley Purdy by their necks, they decided to compromise and "Give them guys just twenty-four hours to clear out of Teton County."

They picked their toughest members to carry the ultimatum to the Binkley place. The poachers, who knew a real showdown when they saw it, made good use of their allotted twenty-four hours. They scraped all the loose elk teeth on hand into a sugar sack and loaded a light camp outfit in a buckboard. When they headed south they carried with them an estimated fifteen hundred sets of elk canines. They reached Los Angeles, but detectives caught up with them and brought them back to Wyoming. A federal judge found them guilty of shooting elk in Yellowstone National Park. Binkley escaped but Purdy served three months at Fort Yellowstone guardhouse. And the Elks Lodge, which would probably as soon forget this fragment of history, disavowed all use of elks' tusks.

By this time Jackson Hole people were becoming truly alarmed about the future of the elk. In fact, there was reason to think elk might disappear from all their remaining range unless something could be done for them right away. Each winter hundreds of them died of starvation. Calves were especially vulnerable. But in an extremely hard winter elk of all ages perished.

One resident I talked with about his recollection of those days was tall, lithe Almer Nelson, who in 1956 retired after thirty-three years as manager of the National Elk Refuge. Nelson came to Jackson Hole at the age of six when his family moved out from Michigan. He recalled especially the harsh winter of 1908–9. "Elk were dying all around us," he said. "There was a mass meeting in the clubhouse in town. Ranchers volunteered to donate hay and others donated their labor. Then they petitioned the governor for emergency relief for the elk."

In spite of all they could do, nearly half of the estimated sixteen thousand elk wintering around Jackson Hole that year died. And the following winter was another bad one for the elk.

A starving elk is no respecter of haystacks. And ranchers, no matter how much they wanted the elk fed, needed the hay to winter their livestock. "Ranchers would make their boys sleep in the haystacks to scare the elk away," Nelson said. "They yelled at the elk and rattled tin cans with bolts in them and the elk would run off a little ways. But they were starving and they wouldn't stay away from the hay for long."

Soon people in other communities and other states across the country were to hear about the elk of Jackson Hole, last of the large herds of American elk. Organized feeding of hay to the Jackson Hole elk had begun in the winter of 1906–7 on Willow Creek, near Pinedale, where a couple of hundred elk were snowbound. The U. S. Forest Service donated hay, and state game wardens hauled it to the elk. Following the mass meeting in Jackson Hole, the state of Wyoming made a $5000 emergency appropriation to buy hay in what was really the first major effort at winter-feeding the animals.

Two years later when the elk were again dying of

winter starvation, Wyoming people took their request all the way to Washington. Congress appropriated $20,000 for more emergency elk rations to feed five to seven thousand elk crowded onto seven feeding grounds across the valley. Meanwhile, Congress decided the elk problem merited a full investigation. The Bureau of Biological Survey dispatched biologist E. A. Preble to Jackson Hole. When he returned from Wyoming he made such a strong case for the elk that Congress, on August 10, 1912, passed a bill authorizing a federal refuge for the indigent elk, and the following March appropriated $50,000 to begin the project.

With this the Department of Agriculture bought 1760 acres of private lands in the winter range of the elk on the edge of Jackson. A beginning had been made on one of the government's earliest efforts to help wildlife. Another 1000 acres was promptly withdrawn from the public domain to enlarge the elk refuge.

Into the job in 1912 as the first manager of the National Elk Refuge went the former Wyoming game warden, D. C. Nowlin, who had been working for several years to help save the starving elk. Nowlin held this refuge post until his retirement in 1923.

In 1925 the Izaak Walton League staged a national fund-raising campaign, to which even school children contributed pennies, for starving elk and raised $36,000. This paid for another 1760 acres of winter elk range. In 1935 Congress authorized expenditures which brought the National Elk Refuge up to its present size of 23,000 acres.

Over the following years the refuge staff built an elk-tight, eight-foot-high drift fence across the south and west sides of the big refuge to keep the elk out of town. The fence which guides the animals to their winter handout is open to the north so elk may come and go in that direction as they please.

The refuge hires twelve extra men in summer to help produce the 2500 tons of mixed grass and legume hay grown on 1480 acres in Mormon Row. Waters of the

Gros Ventre River are ditched in to irrigate the hay during
the short growing season. As part of the cooperative agreement, the Wyoming Game and Fish Commission makes
the hay and hauls it to the twelve sheds scattered across
the refuge lowlands.

An elk eats an average eleven pounds of hay a day
during the refuge feeding period. "We spend the weeks
ahead of the feeding season getting ready," the refuge
manager once explained. "Sleds and harness have to be
repaired and checked, the teams have to be shod." The
feeding gets under way gradually, usually beginning by
early January.

"We load the bales onto our twenty-four-foot by eight-
foot sleds," said Means, "and usually have to leave room
for the passengers. We have been out feeding with temperatures down to fifty-four degrees below zero. That's
when feeding is most important." To make the elk do more
of their own work in winter, the refuge managers leave
part of the hay crop spread out in the fields. At first, they
left it standing for the elk to harvest, but too many of the
leaves were lost. The answer has been to pick it up with
roll balers, then leave the bales in the field without tying
them.

In an average winter the refuge staff feeds 7500 elk,
about half the total herd. Another fourth of the herd is
scattered over eight areas where the State of Wyoming
feeds them, and a fourth of the elk will not come into any
of the feeding areas.

If the elk herd of Jackson Hole is to be managed wisely
and kept healthy over a long period of time, hunting is
almost as important as winter feeding. Said Wyoming big-
game biologist, Chester C. Anderson, "Control of elk by
hunting offers the best answer to the long-range management of the herd and their range."

Jurisdiction over the elk herd belongs to the Wyoming
Game and Fish Commission. But 97 percent of the land
on which they live is in federal ownership. This brings in
the National Park Service, the National Forest Service and

the Fish and Wildlife Service that is responsible for the thirty-seven-square-mile National Elk Refuge. Several years ago these four agencies organized a cooperative committee. Their biologists studied the movements of the migrating elk and the vegetative conditions on the watersheds. And in their meetings the Advisory Council for this group works out recommendations for managing the elk in Jackson Hole. This idea brought all the agencies together to pool their knowledge and resources in managing the Jackson Hole elk herd.

The agencies concerned with the elk herd now agree that it should be held below a total of fifteen thousand animals. With more elk than this in the herd even the summer range may deteriorate. Yet the elk add new members to their herd at the annual rate of eighteen to thirty-five calves per hundred cows.

From long experience the wildlife technicians know how many elk the hunters will take each year from the total herd. In 1961 the hunter kill, from the herd of 14,000 elk, was 2418. Regulations can be easily changed if there is a need to change the size of the herd, its distribution, or even the sex ratio of the adults.

Professional wildlife managers shudder a little at the feeding that has been taking place all these years on the National Elk Refuge. The wildlife manager is actually a habitat manager. He manipulates environmental factors to make an area support as many wild creatures of desirable species as it will on a long-time basis. But he wants the whole plan to retain its natural flavor. To him the very necessity for putting wild creatures on the public dole to get them through the winter is an admission of failure.

The biologist is concerned about the long-range effect of artificial feeding on the natural development of the species. Of all the deer, the elk are the most easily domesticated. Sustained on handouts they are likely to lose their ancestral willingness to go out on their own in search of food. Nobody knows what will be the ultimate effect of this program on the strength and vitality of the Jackson Hole elk herd.

What would the elk herd be like without winter feeding on the refuge? Almer Nelson once told me there might be a few scattered around and there might not. "There might," said the refuge manager, "be five hundred or so." The last big herd of elk on the American continent would be reduced to a remnant that a sudden natural disaster might eliminate.

Refuge manager Larry Means told me he has some fifteen hundred elk each year which do not attempt to leave the refuge in spring to go back into the mountains. These may be the smartest elk of all, or they may be the laziest, or both. "If we leave them here," Means said, "and relax, it won't be many years before we have a real herd down here the year around."

The lazy elk that lose their migratory tendencies should, like their more natural-acting cousins, go back and harvest their own summer food. Instead, they invade ranchlands and make inroads on the hay being grown to feed the elk during the next winter. One solution has been the "elk drive," in which some forty horsemen from around Jackson Hole set the elk to moving slowly. Driving elk is not the world's easiest assignment, but it can be done. The secret is taking it easy. If the horsemen take their time and give the elk plenty of room, they can usually drive at least 75 percent of them up into the hills. Strangely enough, no matter how tame the elk become during the winter, those that return to the mountains go wild again. Larry Means says, "They won't let you within half a mile in summer."

Normally, the bulls are the first to go back up the mountains. They leave in April. Then the cows will work their way out of the refuge, followed by the lazy spike-horned bulls. When the cows depart between mid-April and mid-May, they are heavy with calves which will be born on the way to the high country. Favorite calving grounds are the open sagebrush of Antelope Flats and The Potholes in Grand Teton National Park.

As soon as the calves are strong enough the cows move

higher up the slopes, following the receding snow line.

Later in the summer they begin to congregate and work back down into the valleys. By September again, with the hint of winter in the air and the aspen yellow on the mountain slopes, the elk will once more be headed south toward Jackson Hole and hay.

Success for the Wild Geese

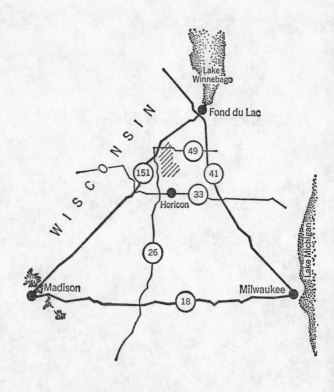

Horicon National Wildlife Refuge

9

On many an autumn day back on the farm I would hesitate in my corn-cutting labors to watch out of sight a high-flying formation of Canada geese. Wild geese were, and still are, birds to kindle wanderlust. They had seen a world the farm boy only dreamed of seeing. They had come from a vast, lonely and mysterious region somewhere to the north, and the winds of the wilderness were in their wings.

Of all the wild geese the best-known are the Canada geese, the "honkers," with their long black necks and white cheeks. Various subspecies of them range, in season, from the Arctic Ocean to the Gulf of Mexico, from the Atlantic to the Pacific. Said ornithologist Arthur Cleveland Bent when writing of the Canada goose, "It is so wary, so sagacious, and so difficult to outwit that its pursuit has always fascinated the keen sportsman and taxed his skill and his ingenuity more than any other game bird."

Around these great birds in recent times revolves one of the outstanding success stories in man's effort to manage wildlife. Bird watchers, hunters and tractor-mounted farm boys see more Canada geese with each passing year. Behind this is a story that makes the waterfowl biologist stand a little taller in his waders.

From all over the country, in each of the four major waterfowl flyways, there are reports of success in increasing the populations of Canada geese and establishing flocks of them in new areas. On Mattamuskeet National Wildlife Refuge in North Carolina there were 10,000 geese during the winter of 1942. By 1959 peak numbers had reached 139,000. At Swan Lake National Wildlife Refuge in Missouri 2000 geese came for the winter of 1942, but by 1955 their numbers were up to 133,500.

But perhaps no Canada geese anywhere are better understood than one segment of those that travel the Mississippi Flyway.

Waterfowl biologists learned from banding studies that the Canada geese using the Mississippi Flyway are not all one big inseparable mass of birds. Instead they are divided into three populations, each with its own flyway within the Mississippi Flyway. Each population originates from a separate breeding ground and has its own distinct wintering area.

Within the Mississippi Flyway the Eastern Prairie Flock nests west of Ft. Severn on Hudson Bay and migrates down the Red River Valley. These geese winter largely on the Swan Lake National Wildlife Refuge in Missouri.

Another group called the TVA Flock occupies a nesting ground lying somewhere in the James Bay area. These geese travel down through Michigan and Ohio to winter in the Tennessee Valley reservoirs, especially the Wheeler National Wildlife Refuge in northern Alabama.

The third major population of geese in this flyway is called the Mississippi Valley Flock, perhaps the group that has been subject to more concentrated research than any other large population of Canada geese. This flock nests in a great triangular patch of tundra lying between the Severn and Kinoje rivers on the southwest edge of Hudson Bay. More than 90 percent of them winter on two areas, the Horseshoe Lake–Crab Orchard area of southern Illinois, and the Horicon National Wildlife Refuge about fifty miles northeast of Madison in southern Wisconsin.

How did these two refuge areas 475 miles apart become two great wintering locations for geese? Historically, geese of this flock had scattered all down the Mississippi Valley to the Gulf of Mexico during fall and winter months. Within a brief span of years their traditional migration patterns have been changed, their age-old wintering habits altered.

Their nesting territory is an expanse of inhospitable wetlands so distant and remote that men have still not threatened to destroy it. Many waterfowl biologists believe there is room on the northern nesting grounds for far more geese.

Yearling geese returning to these grounds may already have chosen their lifelong mates, although they will not nest until the following year. Once the pair chooses its territory and builds the nest, the goose lays five or six eggs. Although the gander refuses to help with the twenty-eight to thirty days of incubation duties, he is never far from his mate. At the slightest hint of danger he lowers his head, moves it snake-like from side to side and issues warning hisses which the intruder had best heed. A glancing blow from a flying gander has been known to knock a man from the saddle of a horse.

The family of geese has strong ties from the beginning. They stay close to each other. When swimming, they are usually in single file, with the gander in the lead, the goose at the rear, and all the goslings paddling along between. In late summer, as the young begin to feather out, the adults molt. These are critical weeks when they must hide for safety because they can no longer fly. But by early September both young and old are ready.

Family groups shift about and congregate. Some of them make short lateral migrations. Others lift into the sky and head directly southward without ceremony. Out of the north the old travelers lead their families over highways, farms and cities. Even on the wintering grounds they stay together in family groups. These geese will travel south eight hundred miles or more before they reach Horicon. There they see below them great flocks of their kind coaxing them from the sky. And once the geese have

settled into this wildlife refuge they may find the living so
good that they outstay their welcome.

In 1941 when the Fish and Wildlife Service purchased
the 21,000-acre Horicon National Wildlife Refuge there
were few who envisioned its future importance to migrating geese. By the late 1940s, however, waterfowl biologists wanted to spread out the goose populations along the
Mississippi Flyway. At Horicon they were beginning to
plant cereal crops in a special effort to attract the geese.
By the fall of 1949 more than 10,000 geese were stopping
at Horicon to rest, and two years later their numbers had
jumped to 100,000. Some even stayed on through the
harsh winter months.

Suddenly Horicon had become one of the country's outstanding Canada-goose areas, with the build-up beginning
in mid-September and reaching its peak early in November. By 1960 the geese had become such an attraction that
200,000 people were flocking to the refuge to see them.
Along State Highway 49, which cuts across the refuge
from east to west, traffic backed up for miles and the State
Police called on civil defense workers to help keep it moving. Eventually the State Highway Department solved the
problem by building two miles of wide parking berms on
either side of the highway. Here, visitors can sometimes
see as many as thirty thousand Canada geese, some feeding at a distance of thirty yards. And frequently they may
see a dozen great white whistling swans that have stopped
for a few days. Among the swans, geese and shore birds
are always a variety of ducks. Some big changes have come
to this marsh.

Horicon owes its birth to a glacier. Behind the ancient
Wisconsin ice sheets stood a lake covering fifty square
miles. Over countless centuries it gradually filled with silt
and decaying vegetation. Advancing age changed it from
lake to marsh. But it still measures fourteen miles from
north to south and two to three miles across.

White settlers, not quite satisfied with what they found
in the Horicon region, made numerous attempts to change

the marsh to their liking. They dammed the stream and recreated the lake, then drained the lake again and finally drained the marsh as well. The peat soils dried and fires set in and burned for years at a time. What was needed to turn the area back into choice wildlife habitat was to put the water back on the land.

Through the region from north to south ran the old Main Ditch built by the drainage engineers. The refuge managers installed a water-control gate at the lower end of the ditch and soon had water spreading again from the ditch out over the flatlands. Meanwhile the Wisconsin Conservation Department had purchased 10,857 acres on the southern end of Horicon Marsh. The state and federal refuges lie adjacent to each other. Both had been a dream of local sportsmen for many years.

With water back on the marsh, smartweed and millet germinated and once more began to provide waterfowl with fall foods. Today, at Horicon, you can see wide areas of such emergent vegetation, broken by irregular bodies of open water and uplands. And the meeting of the various vegetative types provides the edge effect which creates attractive living conditions for a wide variety of wildlife.

For the geese, there are green crops—three thousand acres of corn, wheat and small grain. Sharecroppers grow it and receive a third of the crop in payment. The rest is left standing for wildlife.

"Twenty years ago," I was told at the refuge some years ago, "the hunter who shot a wild goose around here got his picture in the paper, and on the front page." In 1958, however, hunters around the edge of Horicon took an unbelievable fifteen thousand geese. But the following autumn the kill climbed to twenty-five thousand.

These heavy kills were now lending emphasis to a basic objection some serious conservationists had long held about refuges for geese. *The Auk,* official publication of the American Ornithologists' Union, summed up the hazards in its issue of July 1962. The organization's 1961 Committee on Bird Protection reported, "The federal and state refuge programs generally have been of great importance in the production, conservation and sound management of birds." But the report went on to state that acute problems were developing in some areas of goose concentration, especially where there is a combination of abundant artificially provided food and hunting. Geese were noticeably altering their patterns of migration and wintering behavior because of the refuges. The noted conservationists on the committee were concerned because, "These artificial concentrations could endanger the security of certain races and segments of the goose population."

Referring to both Horicon and Horseshoe Lake, the committee added that, "The birds are held in large numbers with a concentrated food supply in a limited area, often until after the instinct for further southward migration has passed. These areas then become the terminus of the migration, and these geese and their young attract others so that the birds build up in surprising numbers in a restricted area. A slaughter of birds follows and too often with high crippling loss. There is always the threat of serious over-harvest under such situations." Solution to the problem, added the committee, must rest heavily on leadership from the Fish and Wildlife Service.

If there was one place where people were not particularly happy about the Wisconsin development, it was down in the southern tip of Illinois. Illinois biologists had been among the first to learn that they could manipulate the Canada-goose flocks. The goose story had begun there in 1927.

Illinois waterfowl specialists watched the annual movements of Canada geese along the Mississippi. They patched together what evidence they could assemble about the travels of the birds and decided that offering food and protection might influence geese to stay a few weeks longer in Illinois. So in 1927, the Illinois Department of Conservation purchased 3500 acres of Mississippi River bottomland in the southwestern tip of the state. The heart of this new state area was an ancient oxbow lake which nature had cut off from the main channel. The lake, called Horseshoe Lake, was filled only during the wet seasons when the river overflowed. The lake bed covered 1200 acres.

One of the first things the Illinois conservation workers did was build a dam across the south end of Horseshoe Lake, to make it a year-around body of water. Next they began planting corn, wheat and grass on the island in the middle of the lake. Before many years passed there was gratifying evidence that the idea was going to work. In fact, Illinois was about to hit the Canada-goose jackpot.

Geese began abandoning the sandbars and islands and filtering into this new area of abundant food. Hunting clubs sprang up around the state area. Each new hunting season brought thousands of waterfowlers, many of whom had never before shot at a goose and knew little about the lore and background of the sport. Around Horseshoe Lake the twelve-gauge brigade held the river bottoms under siege. By 1939 the goose kill in the area was big enough to have conservation authorities, both state and federal, worried.

Where was the wary, sagacious goose that Bent had said was so difficult to outwit? Harold C. Hanson, waterfowl biologist and a specialist in Canada geese for the Illinois Natural History Survey, pointed out that, "The acute wariness that adult geese normally possess seems to be mostly an acquired trait." When the season opened around this state area, the confused birds passed repeatedly before the pits, apparently slow to learn. It was a rare thing when a hunter left Cairo without his limit of geese. Half of the Canada geese in the Mississippi Valley were eventually wintering in southern Illinois. The kill mounted, and elsewhere in the flyway waterfowlers grumbled. Farther down the Mississippi a Canada goose was an increasingly rare sight.

With goose populations low, the hunting season of 1945 brought a climax to the Illinois story. In the first five days of the season five thousand geese were killed around Horseshoe Lake. That did it. The season was quickly closed. And, in spite of the grumbling, the season was closed the following year throughout the flyway. In 1947, the President of the United States and the governor of Illinois agreed to close eighteen thousand acres around Horseshoe Lake to the shooting of wild geese.

This proved another point to the watchful waterfowl biologists. By controlling the total number of birds taken by hunters, they could rebuild goose populations rapidly. The populations began to climb. Obviously, the Canada-goose flocks could be seriously overhunted, and any future management program would have to take this into account. Unlike ducks, which have a major population turnover each year, the geese do not begin to breed until two years old and they normally continue to nest for five or six years.

What most waterfowl biologists wanted to see was the huge southern Illinois flock broken up into smaller and more widely scattered flocks. In 1947 the Fish and Wildlife Service was given jurisdiction over the Crab Orchard National Wildlife Refuge, which helped to spread out the Horseshoe Lake concentration. This refuge, near Carbondale, Illinois, about fifty miles to the north, covers 45,000 acres and produces several thousand acres of grain and pasture annually. By 1953 the population on Crab Orchard had climbed from nothing to forty-eight thousand wintering geese.

Illinois also had created two additional state areas in southern Illinois, the Union County and Mermet refuges. Illinois poured two million dollars into its goose project over the years.

But now Horicon was short-stopping the Illinois-bound geese up in Wisconsin. Geese that once traveled to the Gulf were no longer reaching southern Illinois in time for the hunting season, if at all. Because a migratory bird population is not the exclusive property of any state, there was obviously a need for some fair plan for controlling the kill, in both Wisconsin and Illinois.

Establishing the waterfowl hunting regulations is a tedious, confusing business that sometimes leads to bitter argument. Because migratory birds are a federal responsibility, the Fish and Wildlife Service must play a major role. But the state administrators come into the picture in annual meetings of the Flyway Council. They gather and argue about how many ducks and geese there really are, what would be the sound number to allow hunters to take, how long the seasons should be and when they should fall. And each state is normally, and perhaps understandably, looking out for its own. This Flyway Council has its staff of technicians, and the technicians have a goose subcommittee. In this technical group are perhaps the world's best specialists on the Canada goose. These committees, working together and meeting with Fish and Wildlife Service technicians, decided that the Mississippi Valley population of Canada geese should be stabilized at 300,000 birds.

Research, much of it originating with Harold Hanson in Illinois, now offered them several tools with which to manage the goose populations. In 1960 Hanson and George Arthur, another Illinois waterfowl biologist, had eighteen years of age and sex-ratio data compiled on the goose flock. They could now predict the number of females going north each spring and even forecast accurately what percentage of them would raise young. From here it was an easy step to predict the annual production, the size of the flock, and the number of young birds they could expect back in the fall. Goose management was becoming more and more an exact science.

They knew also from data collected during hunting seasons that reducing the population more than 25 percent by hunting brought losses greater than the flock could replace the following nesting season.

In 1960 the technicians knew the goose flock was considerably short of the 300,000 birds they wanted in it.

They suggested limiting the kill to 12 percent of the total geese. To control the reduction of the flock called for a quota system in both Illinois and Wisconsin. In 1960, the first year the system was in effect, Wisconsin was allowed seven thousand geese around the Horicon area. Illinois, because of its longer history and greater contribution in building the flock, was permitted to take fourteen thousand.

But so early did the geese come winging into Horicon that year that hunters took one thousand a day and their shooting was wrapped up within a week. The season closed amid a barrage of hunter complaints that added up to the speculation that the full-time professional waterfowl biologists didn't know what they were talking about when they said there had been a thousand geese a day killed.

What's more, the refuge workers and state employees on the adjacent area had to contend with complaints from surrounding farmers. The geese liked Horicon and they stayed a couple of months longer than anyone thought they might. They fanned out fifteen miles or more over surrounding grain fields and feasted while disgruntled farmers kept the refuge phone busy with demands that the staff "Come over here and get your geese." The best the refuge manager could suggest was that they build a goose-frightening device by hanging a fertilizer bag over a steel fence post.

As the Mississippi Valley goose flock increased, biologists began to see hints that there might be limits beyond which they could not increase the numbers of geese. Wintering-ground investigations were revealing that the flock's age ratio was changing. With greater concentrations of birds on the wintering grounds, their average age was greater, perhaps a hint that the geese themselves, by some little-understood natural control, might level off their populations. The waterfowl biologists, however, viewed the future of the Canada goose as a bright spot in the waterfowl picture.

Meanwhile there had been another goose-management

project developing over the years. An idea that had fascinated waterfowl managers was that they might build breeding flocks of geese where none existed before. If so, goose populations could be increased and the birds encouraged to occupy whole new territories. This idea began on Seney National Wildlife Refuge with 330 semi-wild, pinioned geese in 1936. The young they produced went south in winter but came back to Seney in Michigan's Upper Peninsula in spring. Seney now produces eight hundred to a thousand goslings annually, while other refuges and numerous state areas turn out smaller numbers.

This is what has happened to the majestic Canada goose. Because he responds readily to the efforts made in his behalf on the wildlife refuges, he exists in a planned economy. If you should pass along Highway 49 in the fall, take time to pull from the road and watch the geese. Not many years ago they were absent from this rural Wisconsin scene. The methods men have used to bring them back here can and will be practiced in other places.

The Whooping Crane's
Last Stand

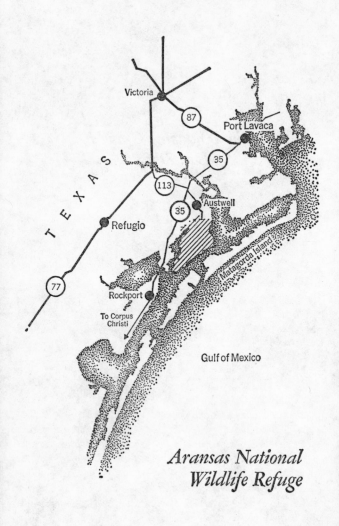

Victoria

(87)

Port Lavaca

(35)

(113)

Austwell

(35)

T E X A S

Refugio

Matagorda Island

(77)

Rockport

To Corpus
Christi

Gulf of Mexico

*Aransas National
Wildlife Refuge*

10

Faint wheel marks led us through dense stands of black-jack oak, across open fields, then out on a point from which we could look down over the tidal flats. Here the world's few remaining whooping cranes would spend the coming winter.

The giant cranes were off somewhere in the distant northern wilderness, presumably nesting and perhaps adding a few individuals to their little remnant flock. But there was still abundant wildlife scattered over this sprawling refuge. Off in the distance a row of pastel-pink roseate spoonbills stood in the shallow water. The dashing scavenger caracaras were abundant, and so were the scissor-tailed flycatchers.

Almost within sight of refuge headquarters we saw four wild turkeys, and before completing the thirty-mile circuit we counted fifty whitetail deer in the heat of the day when deer are usually bedded down in the shade. "So many people automatically think of whooping cranes when Aransas National Wildlife Refuge in mentioned," the refuge manager once told me, "that they forget we have a lot of other wildlife here. In fact," he added, taking obvious pleasure in the wild creatures around him, "I've never been on a refuge anywhere that had more indigenous wildlife for people to see."

But it is the whooping crane, *Grus americana*, that

brings people to this refuge from all over the world. He is
the tallest of all birds native to North America. He stands
almost five feet high and one of his footprints in the mud
measures seven inches across. He has a seven-foot wingspread and sometimes, during migration, flies so high he is
out of sight from ground observers. The windpipe is longer
than the bird himself and more than two feet of it coils
behind the breast bone. The whoopers' "ker-looo" call of
alarm, which can be heard as far as two miles away, once
reminded wilderness settlers of an Indian war cry.

The adult has pure-white feathers, a red crowned head
and black-tipped wings. The young birds are rust-colored
but during their first winter the reddish coloring wears
away and spring finds them as white as their parents.

Whooping cranes mate for a lifetime. The families stay
together, with the young coming southward on their first
journey in the company of their elders. Even when they
reach the wintering grounds they continue to live together
in family territories, and not until the courtship dancing begins in late winter will the old birds drive their young
away.

The whooping crane is probably the world's most seriously watched bird. It is also one of the rarest and one of
the least likely to succeed. If the Aransas National Wildlife
Refuge had not been established, the whooping crane
would doubtless have disappeared by now.

These birds, wild of spirit, demand great open spaces.
Once, when there was space aplenty, whooping cranes
nested across the north-central part of what is now the
United States and all the way north into the arctic. They
nested in wetlands in what the white man later labled Illinois, Iowa and the Dakotas. And in winter they fanned
out along the coastal marshes all the way from New Jersey
around to Texas.

One should not think that whooping cranes darkened
the skies like passenger pigeons, or came south in great
numbers like the ducks and geese. Naturalists tell us that
most likely the whooping crane never was an abundant

bird, at least not for the last million years, which, one must admit, takes the story back quite a while. The whooper, even before he felt the pressure of spreading human populations, exerted certain pressures on his own kind. Under ideal conditions a family of them requires four hundred to five hundred acres of tidal marsh for its wintering grounds and will drive away any other whooping cranes that dare invade its territory. Likewise, they spread out widely over the nesting grounds.

Nor will they stick around when men are nearby. To approach a wintering whooping crane within half a mile is a rare experience. With great resounding alarm calls the bird takes off at the first sight of human invasion.

Here then was a bird which in the early 1800s was suddenly subjected to the advance of people, first across its ancient wintering grounds, and eventually into its nesting territories. Unlike the bobwhite or the whitetail deer, the whooping crane never accepted this energetic two-legged creature that plowed the land, burned the fields, cleared forests and fenced the range.

It began to seem even before 1920 that the whoopers could no longer be saved. In 1923 one influential national magazine stated flatly that the whooping cranes were gone. But along the Platte River in Nebraska amateur observers could still see a few of the big birds every October and November as they traveled southward from nesting to wintering grounds. The whooping cranes themselves had not given up, at least not yet.

The only known remaining wintering ground was along the tidal flats of the Blackjack Peninsula on the east coast of Texas. In 1936 the National Audubon Society, cooperating with the Fish and Wildlife Service, censused the whoopers on their wintering grounds and could find only eighteen. With encouragement from many quarters, the federal government the following year established the Aransas National Wildlife Refuge, which today covers 47,261 acres.

One of the most important things the National Audu-

bon Society did in behalf of the hard-pressed whooping
cranes was to assign its experienced ornithologist Robert
L. Allen to ferret out still unknown facts in the bird's life
history. Allen had already won widespread respect for his
work on the roseate spoonbills. His efforts and hardships
in the next several years on behalf of the whooping crane
were monumental.

There was so little understood about the whooping
crane that Allen was faced with several tasks all at once.
What were they eating there on the Texas coast? Were
eating habits and territorial behavior important factors in
limiting their numbers? Were there ways to supplement
their natural food supplies? And what of their nesting territory? No one even knew where the last of these birds
spent the summer, and consequently their nesting area
could not be protected against dangers that might threaten
it. There was plenty for Bob Allen to do.

He began to watch the big birds. Eventually he compiled a list of foods, both animal and vegetable, consumed
regularly by the whoopers. He made extensive notes on
their behavior and how they defended their territories.

Manager of the Aransas National Wildlife Refuge when
this work got under way was Julian Howard, who later
moved on to manage the Wichita Mountains National
Wildlife Refuge in Oklahoma. It was while talking with
him there that I learned some of the early steps taken to
bolster the dwindling whooper population. Allen and Howard made a pioneering, but not highly successful, effort
to produce young whoopers in captivity.

Allen knew, when assigned to the whooper project by
the National Audubon Society, that two injured whooping
cranes were in captivity. One was a bird known to be at
least fourteen years old. He, or she, and no one knew for
certain which, was in the Audubon Park Zoo in New
Orleans. Hopefully, they called this bird Josephine. Josephine was the only surviving member of a small flock of
non-migratory whooping cranes that had perished in a
hurricane in the Louisiana marshes. The other captive bird

had been shot by a hunter, was blind in one eye, had a crippled wing and was known to be at least ten years old. He was held by a gun club in Gothenburg, Nebraska, in a cage with assorted birds of lesser stature. He was known as Old Devil for his tendency to punish the other birds. Old Devil eventually became known, also hopefully, as Pete.

Bob Allen and the refuge staff were more interested in preserving wild birds than caged ones. But the whooping crane was so close to oblivion that any addition to the ranks would be welcomed. Consequently Allen wanted to bring these two captive birds together at Aransas. The cranes would need a suitable place to live, so Allen and Howard laid out a 150-acre plot, to be closed in with a nine-foot fence. Within this whooping crane enclosure were both the typical tidal flat in which the wintering birds fed, and a section of fresh-water marsh that came as close as the coast of Texas could to duplicating the whooper's northern summering range.

Now the scene was set for a drama that was destined to fall short of expectations. "I got more gray hairs over whooping cranes," Howard recalled, "than I did over my children." In the fall of 1948, Josephine and Pete were brought to Texas by truck and turned loose in the big enclosure. There was nothing to do then but wait.

The biggest question of all was answered in December. Howard immediately flashed word to Bob Allen, who was back home in Tavernier, Florida. The two whoopers had performed their strange and impressive prenuptial dance. Pete, in fact, was a male, and Josephine a female. Jubilation.

"Toward spring," Howard told me, "they danced more and more frequently. In April we began to notice that when they came up to the fence at feeding time for their corn, they no longer came together." On April 30, when one of the birds was seen crouching in the marsh while the other came up to feed, the refuge workers entered the enclosure and found a nest that measured about ten inches high and five to six feet across. In the middle was a single, large, buff-colored egg with brown spots on it. The following day a second whooping-crane egg was placed beside it.

Meanwhile refuge workers had built a blind on a twenty-foot-high tower from which Allen could observe the nesting birds. This was the first opportunity an ornithologist ever had to make close-up observations of the nesting behavior of the vanishing whooping crane. Allen spent all of the daylight hours every day inside the blind studying the birds through a spotting scope. Minute by minute he made notes of their activities, which he later described in his book *On the Trail of Vanishing Birds*.

But tragedy stalked the whoopers. There had always been a serious question in the minds of both Allen and Howard about the fertility of the eggs produced by these aging birds. Finally, after twenty-four days of incubation, the birds broke the eggs and abandoned the nest. "The eggs were both infertile," Howard said.

It was hardly a month later when refuge workers were awakened at dawn by the loud calls of one of the whoopers. Howard dressed and raced out to the enclosure. In the back of his mind was the nagging knowledge that Pete had not been eating properly in recent days.

As he approached the pen he saw Josephine still whooping in what he interpreted as distress calls. Pete was nearby, lying on his back dead in the shallow water.

But Howard had still one more idea. Off in a remote corner of the refuge was a fine big whooper named Crip. This bird, probably injured by gunfire during his last migratory flight southward, had not gone north in the spring in 1948. Howard obtained authorization from Washington to capture Crip and install him in the enclosure with the pining Josephine. So refuge workers caught the whooper and carried him uninjured to the enclosure.

Shortly the two birds engaged in their prenuptial dance routine. This, I am told, is a sight to remember.

The pageant begins in shallow water when the male

stretches his wings high over his back and bows toward the female as though to ask her, in courtly fashion, if she would care to dance. More than likely she would love to dance, so she struts out beside her mate. He rockets into the air on stiffened legs. He does a half turn, and as he comes down his long beak dips into the water and he whips his head around and throws spray across his shoulder as if tossing salt for luck. The female dances too, bounding up and down with her mate in the shallow water. But the male is the finer dancer of the two and as the spirit engulfs him he seems oblivious to the world except for the female for which he performs. As spring comes on they dance with increasing frequency.

Crip, even with his injured wing, did himself proud in this age-old whooping-crane ballet. Then the birds built their nest and Josephine deposited a single egg. Sometime on the night of May 24 and 25, 1950, the egg chipped; the first whooping crane ever hatched in captivity joined his parents on the Aransas Wildlife Refuge. The parents could hardly have been more pleased than were Howard and Allen, as well as bird students everywhere.

What would happen to this rusty-colored little chick which Bob Allen tried to watch so closely from his nearby observation post? The world was not long in finding out. Events in the little family went smoothly until the third day. Then from the observation post Allen saw the old birds leave the nest. From the way they acted it was plain that "Rusty" was with them, there beside their great feet, hidden in the tangle of grasses.

But other things bothered the observers. Howard joined Allen in the blind and they began to notice with increasing fear the other species around the nest. Howard eliminated an alligator that he felt threatened the safety of the young crane. But most noticeable of all were the raccoons.

Later, the old birds walked a considerable distance from the nest site. When Howard went into the enclosure, the old birds practically ignored him. They showed no sign of having a young bird under their protection; and they didn't. A long search failed to turn up the chick. There were little pieces of shell from which the bird had come but Rusty had disappeared completely. "We think a predator took him," Howard told me. Crip and Josephine, as part of a previous agreement, were taken then to live in the Audubon Park Zoo in New Orleans.

The puzzle that had most consistently defied solution was the exact location of the nesting grounds of the whooping cranes after traveling north each season. From Aransas the birds crossed Texas, Oklahoma, Kansas, Nebraska, and the Dakotas, and flew on into Saskatchewan. But somewhere to the north, the cranes managed to hide themselves while they built their nests and reared their young in the vast unoccupied wilderness.

Wildlife specialists, foresters and bush pilots had kept their eyes open for the flash of white that would lead them to some unknown nesting grounds. Many believed that the nesting area must lie somewhere in the vicinity of Great Slave Lake.

Then in June of 1954 a great fire swept across a section of the Wood Buffalo National Park, which lies partly in the Northwest Territories. Two weary Canadian forestry workers were flying south from that region. Suddenly, one of them spotted a large white bird standing in a shallow pond below. Then he saw a second bird. And there with them was a smaller bird with the young whooping crane's rusty coloring. It was already evening when the excited fliers contacted their headquarters by radio and told biologist William A. Fuller what they had found.

One of the last great mysteries in the life of the continent's tallest bird had been solved. And at the time of the discovery the Canadian government was planning a new railroad that would have penetrated the heart of the last whooping-crane nesting ground. The route was changed to protect the birds. And now even low-flying planes have been forbidden there during the nesting season.

Had it not been for the fact that some of them nested so far to the north in an inhospitable wilderness the whooping cranes would have long since vanished from the list of North American wild creatures. Or if this same flock had spent its winters in some section of the coast more attractive to men than the flat, tidal marshes off the east coast of Texas, it would have yielded its winter quarters by this time to cabanas and neon-lighted roadhouses. Only that fraction of the original whooping-crane population with this fortunate combination of isolated nesting area and remote wintering grounds still has descendants on earth.

Actually, only about eight thousand acres or roughly one sixth of the Aransas refuge is important to the whooping cranes. This is a strip of salt-water flats perhaps a mile wide. These grassy stretches of shallow water provide the birds with blue crabs and other foods that support them. The strip of crane territory reaches down the coast from Mustang Lake a dozen or so miles to Cape Carlos. The muddy deltas of several creeks reach out into the area and provide additional feeding grounds. And across the bay other whooping cranes find wintering territories on Matagorda Island, which is privately owned.

The Intracoastal Waterway reaches up through the whoopers' territory. But the crews of barges operating on the waterway are among the cranes' defenders. At least one barge owner has standing orders for the captain to dismiss any crew member carrying a firearm.

Every year some twenty-five thousand visitors register at the Aransas Refuge. And many of them come during the winter months especially to see the whooping cranes. Some of them, however, are doomed to disappointment. "Some years," said former refuge manager Huyson Johnson, "90 percent of them will see whooping cranes." Usually this is from the big observation platform, because one family of whoopers normally establishes a wintering territory in the flats in front of this platform. "People come long distances to see the birds," said Johnson, "and they get all excited when they spot one. I've seen elderly women jump up and down and squeal like children at sight of a whooping crane." Some years, however, fewer than 30 percent of the winter visitors will spot a whooping crane. Most of the wintering territory is out of bounds for visitors. "The most important thing of all," said Johnson, "is to provide the birds with isolation."

"With a species so close to extinction as the whooping crane," he adds, "every year is significant." During the summer months Johnson's crew of workers do all they can to get the refuge ready for the return of the whooping cranes. For several weeks after the birds first arrive they spend a couple of hours a day feeding in the higher areas along the coast, especially in openings in the scrub oak. So in these openings the refuge workmen keep about a thousand acres mowed. "When they first come in," Johnson said, "they pick up a few acorns, grasshoppers, and snakes in places like this."

The most exciting time of year at Aransas comes with early autumn. "About September 15 to 20," said Johnson, "I find myself down in the whooper areas more and more." Here the refuge manager scans the salt flats and the sky even when he knows it is still too early for the first arrivals. Not until mid-December, when the last of the birds is sure to have reached the coast, does the tension ease. "It's the most helpless feeling in the world, waiting for them," said Johnson, "there's so little you can do." Every time he spots a new arrival the refuge manager places a long-distance call to his superiors directly in Washington. The whole country wants to know what he sees.

Johnson thought the quality of the whoopers' winter foods might have a bearing on nesting success the following season. And because of this he hoped to try some methods of further supplementing their supplies of winter foods. Why, he wondered, do the big birds feed in some of the places they do, and ignore others? What is it, for example, that draws them across the bay to Matagorda Island? Why do they move off for a few days, then return to an area?

Just how effective all these efforts will prove to the

whooping cranes over the long haul is open to question. There is a growing conviction among professional biologists that the whooper, in spite of all the belated concern lavished on him by the remorseful human, is lost, unless some drastic new plan is created to salvage the species. "I am convinced," one biologist in the Fish and Wildlife Service told me, "that it is only a matter of time before the present population meets its doom—as the Louisiana birds did. Either a hurricane on the wintering grounds or a good 'norther' could catch the birds during spring or fall migration and do the trick."

As protection against such a disaster, the Fish and Wildlife Service has begun a new plan, to produce whooping cranes in captivity in an effort to establish new flocks. Some biologists believe it may still be possible to establish an entirely new flock of whooping cranes with new nesting and wintering grounds, and a shorter and less hazardous migration route.

Once a propagation center is established, biologists will travel to the nesting grounds to gather eggs. Early in 1964 the United States and Canada reached an agreement to steal a few eggs annually from whooper nests as soon as the birds lay, hoping they will re-nest. In theory this plan, carried on for thirty years, might create a new flock of thirty captive whoopers plus the production from captive birds. One specialist working in this field tells me, "I believe we can produce an average of four to six young from each captive pair annually. It will take fifteen to twenty birds at best before we could have sufficient birds to establish new colonies and add to the existing population."

Meanwhile, alerted citizens along the whoopers' migration routes will continue to watch anxiously for the big white birds traveling to and from their last wintering grounds on the Texas coast. Few birds in all history have created as much interest or generated the great concern centered on this victim of the changing times.

Valley of the Rescued Swans

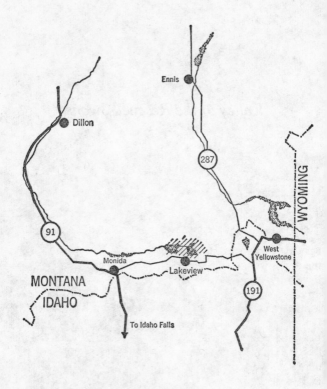

*Red Rock Lakes National
Wildlife Refuge*

Once you have seen a wild trumpeter swan you do not soon forget the experience. These are big, white, powerful birds with a resounding deep-toned call audible across two miles of mountain marshes. And they are wild. Getting near them is seldom a simple task.

I first had a close look at trumpeters on a fine September day when the quaking aspen along the foothills and up the draws were already bright yellow with their fall colors. From the village of West Yellowstone, Montana, I had driven westward on Highway 191 to the dirt road which leads past the Red Rock Lakes National Wildlife Refuge, famous as the home of the trumpeters. I skirted Henry's Lake, which the swans sometimes use for resting during their migratory flights over to Yellowstone. This lake was once the scene of a brief contest between the trumpeters and the armed forces. The U. S. Army wanted the lake area for an artillery practice range. Conservationists rose to defend the swans and the squabble ended in Washington. "The verdict is for the trumpeter swan and against the army," said President Franklin D. Roosevelt. "The army must find a different nesting place."

Across the Continental Divide I began the long descent down into Centennial Valley. For twenty miles there was little sign of human activity except for a temporary logging camp where giant Douglas fir were being dragged down the mountain slopes, and a few herds of white-faced cattle. On the floor of the valley, bands of antelope mixed with the cattle.

Then I could see Upper Lake, the largest body of water in this remote Montana valley, and over along one edge of the lake were two white dots which had to be trumpeter swans, a mile or more away. A few decades earlier this would have been one of the rarest sights in the world of birds. And even now the trumpeters can be seen only in isolated mountain marshes in a few Western states.

There are in the world today seven species of swans, the biggest of waterfowl, graceful, stately birds that have long attracted the attention and admiration of man. Two of these seven swans, the whistler and the trumpeter, are native to North America. Unlike the trumpeter, the smaller whistling swan is frequently seen in large numbers.

Centennial Valley, which lies on the southwestern edge of Montana, along the Idaho border, is wild country where Nature has not yet been bent to the will of man. It is a region of high mountain lakes and fertile marshes walled in by some of the most inhospitable mountains in the Rockies. The valley is sixty miles long and five miles wide and the only road through it is the dirt road I followed. The mailman comes three times a week, and in winters, when temperatures often drop to forty degrees below zero, he comes by snow sled. The local school, when I was last there, had one teacher and one student. In this valley the trumpeter swan, largest of North American waterfowl, made its last stand.

Some hours later I turned north onto a lane leading across a plateau toward the Red Rock River two miles away. Two swans, a quarter of a mile down the stream, turned and began swimming rapidly away as my car approached. Then I could see others resting along the shore and standing in the bulrushes. Those not already on the river moved nervously toward the water.

Some distance to the south were the wooden pilings and remnants of an old bridge. I left the car far back from the river's edge and kept myself hidden as much as possible as I moved down the dry bed of a shallow wash toward the remains of the old bridge. Some of the trumpeters were swimming steadily downstream away from me and a flock of a dozen or more lifted themselves with great commotion of their wings against the water and flew down the valley.

Within a few minutes, after I had hidden among the old bridge timbers, some of the birds on the water began swimming back toward me. Those in the air flew two or three miles south along the river and circled repeatedly out over Blake Slough. Even when they were white specks against the sky I could hear their trumpeting calls rolling back up the valley. Instead of settling on the water downstream, as I expected, they eventually began flying back toward me, lined out in formation at low altitude. Then, with their great wings beating the air noisily, they were flying past my hiding place and I photographed them repeatedly, with the gentle, sage-covered slopes of the Gravelly Mountains for a backdrop.

These swans in front of me on the Red Rock River and around me in the marshes were a large part of all those remaining in the world.

There is evidence that trumpeter swans once wintered in New England and nested as far east as Illinois. Biologist Winston E. Banko, while working with the trumpeter for the Fish and Wildlife Service, searched the history of these birds. "At one time or another in the distant past," he wrote in his fine monograph on the species, "before man first appeared on the North American Continent, trumpeter swans must have occurred commonly within nearly every region of what is now the United States. The advance and retreat of a succession of ice ages determined the distribution and status of this species."

Archaeologists, digging about in the mounds and kitchen middens of prehistoric Indians, found remains of trumpeter swans in such widely scattered areas as Florida, Illinois and Oregon. But this bird, wild by nature, simply gave up as men drained the marshes on which they nested and occupied the regions over which they had migrated. Hunting added speed to their disappearance. The young were considered choice eating. The plumage became an item of commerce. Audubon records the "slaughter" of fifty trumpeter swans by Indians near the point where the Ohio empties into the Mississippi, to obtain skins, "All intended for the ladies of Europe." This traffic in swan skins continued for more than a century.

Then, around the turn of the century, with trumpeters everywhere else gone, people in Centennial Valley found an unusual new business opportunity. Zoological gardens everywhere were eager to own some of the rare trumpeter swans. The going price for a pair of the young, known as cygnets, was seventy-five dollars. Valley residents could capture them easily in September before they had learned to fly. They penned up the cygnets and shipped them out of the village of Monida, Montana, to many parts of the country, and in a strange manner may have helped to save the species.

Within the valley people warned each other that the old birds must be protected. The seed must be saved. But the big, low-flying swans made an easy mark for visiting gunners, who have always come here in autumn for duck hunting. Finally there were so few swans left that the cygnet business was abandoned.

The Migratory Bird Treaty Act, passed in 1918, came too late to help the trumpeter much. The damage was done. Hunters still shot the rare swans as "snow geese," until the federal government in later years closed the seasons on snow geese in those states where the trumpeter lived. Later the regulation was changed again to prohibit shooting of all "large white waterfowl" in Idaho, Wyoming and Colorado and in Madison, Gallatin and Beaverhead counties in Montana.

In the year 1912 famed ornithologist E. H. Forbush, writing of the sad plight of the trumpeter swan, said, "Its total extinction is now only a matter of years." "Its trumpeting call," he added, "will soon be locked in the silence of the past." And most people agreed.

Then in the summer of 1919, M. P. Skinner, an employee of the National Park Service, was far back in the wilderness section of Yellowstone, northeast of Lewis Lake. Off in a lagoon was a low island at which Skinner stared in disbelief. There, in plain view, swam a pair of swans. Skinner returned on September 6 of that year. With the adult swans there were now three young cygnets big enough to fly. Here was the first record of the trumpeter breeding in Yellowstone National Park, and one of the few recent instances when it had been seen there.

Conservationists across the country soon knew about the discovery, which raised hopes that the trumpeter might yet be saved. These Yellowstone trumpeters were not birds pushed into the wilderness by the advance of man; they were, instead, birds men had not yet pushed out of the wilderness. This set the Park Service people to searching for still more pairs of trumpeters. They discovered that at least part of the swans sometimes seen in Yellowstone came from Centennial Valley across the mountains.

The single development playing the largest role in the now rare trumpeter's struggle came in 1929. That year Congress approved the Migratory Bird Conservation Act. This authorized the Bureau of Biological Survey to purchase lands for waterfowl refuges. Five years later, in 1934, Congress backed up its intention with money. The trumpeter swan was one of the first birds to benefit. J. N. ("Ding") Darling, then head of the Biological Survey, and J. Clark Salyer II, the young biologist he had chosen to take charge of the refuge system, knew that if the trumpeters were to be saved there must be a refuge for them in the Centennial Valley. And it must be established at once. The executive order that created Red Rock Lakes National Wildlife Refuge was signed in 1935 by President Franklin D. Roosevelt.

At first the refuge boundaries included 22,682 acres, but they were soon extended to make a refuge of 40,000 acres in the trumpeter's historic breeding and wintering grounds, a refuge fifteen miles long and five miles wide between the mountain ranges. Some of this land was already in the public domain, but the most important parts were privately owned by families that homesteaded there. And, as much as they might favor the trumpeters, some of the local people fought last-ditch stands in the courts against having to sell their holdings to the government. Even today some bitterly insist that the government took too much land.

The water system in Centennial Valley is almost ideal for trumpeters. Far up in the Centennial Mountains, to the south and east of the refuge, melting snows form tumbling ice-cold brooks all summer long. A few smaller streams feed into the valley from the Gravelly range on the north. One of the principal streams coming down from the Continental Divide is Red Rock Creek, which local people have always called "Hell's A'Roarin' Creek." This stream plus Elk Spring Creek and Tepee Creek coming down from the north and Tom Creek and Odell Creek from the south feed water into the marshes and lakes of the refuge. Smallest of the lakes is the 400-acre Swan Lake, nowhere more than ten inches deep. It is so shallow a swan can stand almost anywhere on the bottom if he chooses.

Upper Red Rock Lake is the largest of the lakes. This is also the deepest. It covers 2880 acres and has no islands. Then four miles down the valley is the 1540-acre Lower Red Rock Lake. From this shallow lake protrude hundreds of small islands covered with thick-growing bulrushes. The marshland vegetation, mostly beaked sedge, extends to the very edge of the water. And no timber grows there except for patches of quaking aspen along the south shore of the upper lake. Swans on the lakes can see the countryside for miles around.

In the bottoms of these lakes one finds the secret of their attraction for swans, as well as for the hundreds of lesser scaups which share the waters with the trumpeters. The lake bottoms are fertile black mucklands, incubators for incredible populations of all manner of aquatic ceatures native to high-altitude marshes. There are frogs, toads and polliwogs, and the fry of several kinds of fish. Caddis flies and water beetles live here by the millions. When Winston Banko conducted waterfowl food studies here over a period of several years, he found that during the summer growing season, when the sun warms the shallow marshes, crustaceans and plankton flourish in "unbelievable abundance."

How close had the trumpeters come to their extinction? What did the refuge people have left to work with? An actual head count of trumpeter swans in 1935 revealed that only seventy-three wild trumpeters remained south of the Canadian border.

The first step in helping the shy birds was to eliminate human trespass around the nesting areas. Then grazing was cut back to give the marsh vegetation a chance to return to its wild condition. Meanwhile, the first refuge manager, A. V. Hull, stopped all muskrat trapping in the area because the muskrat houses were Nature's nesting platforms for the swans. Because muskrat numbers were low, refuge workers began constructing artificial nesting platforms in the marsh. This they did in winter by placing a wooden frame on the ice, loading it with marsh hay and equipping it with anchors so it would stay in place once the ice melted in spring. The swans used the man-made platforms until the muskrats eventually returned.

There were coyotes in Centennial Valley, a lot of them, and the waterfowl biologists, convinced at the time that coyotes were a major predator on swans, reduced the coyote populations.

Winter months are hardest on the swans. The freeze-up comes early in the high country where they live. The mountain marshes are solid with ice and snow for half a year or more. By the time winter descends on Centennial Valley, swans and other waterfowl have already fed heavily on their store of natural foods. The refuge was scarcely a year old in the winter of 1936–37 when the manager decided that the swans would need some help to get through the winter. Wildlife managers frown on winter feeding under most circumstances and label it "unnatural." Let the creatures shift for themselves, and the strongest come through to keep the race going. But it was another story now with the swans; they were hard-pressed for survival and their environment was no longer a natural one. Without winter feeding some of the rare swans would starve. The search for food might force others beyond the protective boundaries of the refuge. And no trumpeter could be spared. The winter feeding program begun that year became a permanent cold-weather chore. "Twice a week from early November until mid-March we feed them small grain," refuge biologist Ged Devan told me. "We scatter wheat and barley into the water from a boat."

The refuge has two small lakes that never freeze over. These are the only places where the swans can feed in winter. There is the Widow's Pool or Culver's Pond, which is spring fed and has a year-around water temperature of forty-one degrees. It was the only open pond on the refuge for many years. Mrs. Culver once charged visiting fishermen to fish this thirty-acre pond for its huge native brook trout. "Sometimes they came so big," I was told in Centennial Valley, "that you couldn't hide one in a hip boot." One-pounders are more the rule in recent years. This is also one of the few remaining places where hope exists for saving the rare Montana grayling.

In the man-made MacDonald Pond, springs keep the water temperature at fifty-nine degrees, a year-around heated swimming pool for trumpeters. "We feed in both ponds," Devan explained, "and never less than thirty bushels at a feeding. Even this doesn't make the swans tame. They leave when we come with the feed, then later in the day come back when we're gone." There is no doubt that the winter feeding, which now consumes scarcely 750 bushels of grain a year, enables the Red Rock Lakes refuge to support more of the endangered swans than could otherwise have lived here.

Towering above the refuge headquarters is Sheep Mountain, a convenient 9000-foot-high perch for those who want to look down on swans. Here, beginning in mid-May each year, refuge personnel go twice a week to count the swans. They carry with them a twenty-power spotting scope with which they scan the entire marsh, counting the birds and verifying the territories they occupy.

Then in early June a pilot-biologist comes down from Fish and Wildlife Service Regional Headquarters in Portland, Oregon, to conduct an aerial survey. Once each year, usually in early September, there is the annual National Aerial Trumpeter Swan Survey. The locations in which the swans live are already known and they are close together, so the entire task is completed in four days. The Fish and Wildlife Service pilot-biologist lands on a grass strip near the refuge headquarters. He picks up the refuge biologist as well as naturalists from Yellowstone and Grand Teton national parks. On the first of these counts in 1932 they could find only sixty-nine swans left. But the population increased at the rate of about 10 percent a year following establishment of the refuge until biologists now count more than seven hundred trumpeters on their annual tally.

The trumpeter's total length, if you include his lengthy neck, may be five feet, and his great powerful wings stretch six feet from tip to tip. He may weigh more than thirty pounds. Most young trumpeters have light-gray feathers on the head, neck and back. But this is only temporary. Eventually they exchange this stigma of youth for the pure-white uniform of the graceful adults. The big powerful beak is black and so are the web feet and the scaly legs. The eyes, which a decorator would say do not match the rest of the immaculate uniform, are dark brown.

The trumpeter's windpipe has an extra long loop curled back into his breastbone. Nature denied the whistling swan this special loop, so that the bird's call is high-

pitched, and sounds, some say, like "wow-wow-wow." But
the trumpeter carries a bass horn. He sounds a deep and
melodious note across the miles of marsh. Early Eastern
settlers, hearing this call, spoke of the big white birds as
"trompeters" and the name has stayed with them.

As trumpeters gather their food from the bottoms of
shallow ponds and marshes, they will sometimes tip up
their tails to the sky after the fashion of the puddle ducks.
What they are seeking, in addition to aquatic insects and
crustaceans, are the succulent, starch-rich roots of such
aquatics as pondweed, milfoil and white water buttercup.
Later in the winter, with these favored foods in low supply,
they turn to the roots and even the stems and leaves of
almost any aquatic plants available.

Late in winter they spend increasing hours standing in
the snow on the edges of their winter ponds at the Red
Rock Lakes refuge. They call frequently and make re-
peated flights out over the marsh. Eventually they are returning to the ponds only for brief visits to feed. By the
middle of March, with the temperature now often above
freezing, the swans' mating drive reaches its peak. So does
their trumpeting, the heralding of spring, awakening of the
new season and the beginning of a new family.

Winston Banko, who has spent as much time as anyone living and working with the trumpeters, told me the
swans are ready to nest when the ice goes out in May.
These birds are thought to mate for life, pairing off perhaps at the age of three, and building their first nests when
five years old. Trumpeters have been known to live more
than thirty years.

They commonly return to the previous year's nest.
Those building a nest for the first time must search about
for a suitable unoccupied site. Lacking a muskrat house
for a start, the swans construct a platform of their own by
pulling marsh plants and stacking them in piles. This is no
small task; the nest of a trumpeter is often five feet across.
The female adds the finishing touches when she lines the
nest with her down.

What swans' eggs lack in design and color they make up in size. Each of the dull-white eggs weighs three quarters of a pound. The pen, as a female swan is known, usually lays a clutch of six to eight eggs. She does the incubation chores herself while her mate rests and stands guard nearby, ready to sound a warning trumpet call at the sign of trouble. She must sit on her eggs for thirty-five days. Before leaving her nest for any reason she usually takes time first to hide her eggs beneath the down in which they rest.

The young cygnets stay in the nest only long enough for their down to dry. Then they slip into the water with their parents and begin several weeks in which the family is always close together as it feeds and rests in its own territory within the swan community. The family territory may be a quarter of a mile across. The family breaks up the following March, when the parents start a new nesting season.

"Cygnets hatched in June," said Banko, "are ready to fly by early October." Before they can solo, however, they must receive flight instruction from the old birds. It is no easy task for a swan to become airborne. The bird heads into the wind with its neck and head extended, and with a great beating of wings and pushing of feet, gets up and runs over the water at full throttle. His wings slap sharply against the surface of the water. Once aloft, however, the swan regains his composed and graceful demeanor. His feet and legs trail back beneath the tail and the neck is extended.

Landings are a little more graceful and look easier. The swan glides gently downward into the wind and uses his lowered feet against the water to break his speed. Both in the air and on the water swans seem at ease and in their element. It is the transition from one to the other that robs them of their composure.

As their summer feeding grounds begin to freeze, the young cygnets may still not have seen their home from the air. Now the old birds fly ahead of them and eventually

entice the young to follow. Trumpeters in ages past have
made lengthy migrations from summer to winter feeding
grounds, but today's birds make only short seasonal
journeys, or none at all.

As he compiled and studied trumpeter census figures
over the years, Banko began to notice an amazing ability
of the birds to adjust their own populations to their available habitat. During the period from 1936 to 1942, when
the swans were perhaps at their lowest point in history,
74 percent of the paired swans were accompanied by
young birds during the annual census.

From 1951 to 1957, however, when the swans' numbers
were building, only 39 percent of the pairs were accompanied by young. But in this later period also the average
size of the broods was decreasing. Instead of the 3.7 cygnets per pair of adults in the earlier period, the old birds
now had only 2.8 young per pair—a decrease of 24 percent.

But what did remain almost the same during both periods was the number of young swans produced on the refuge each year. Over those years the number of mated
pairs on the refuge had increased 250 percent. Cygnet
production for the two periods, however, had increased
hardly at all. In the earlier period there were 45.4 young
per year on the average and during the latter period 46
young were produced each year.

Could this leveling off of production be due to chance?
The odds, as Banko computed them, are more than two
million to one.

Obviously the swans themselves place some control over
their numbers in a nesting region. As their numbers increase and mated pairs claim available nesting territory, a
growing percentage of the adults are relegated to the ranks
of the non-breeders. The average size of the clutch falls
off. And there may also be a growing percentage of infertile eggs, all somehow controlled, biologists believe, by
the courtship activity in late winter, and related to the
number of adult birds in the flock.

Probably more people see live, wild trumpeters today

in the Targee National Forest than anywhere else. Here, as vacationers drive along the blacktop highway toward Yellowstone National Park, they see the big white swans often in plain view in the Island Park area of Idaho. The greatest numbers of trumpeters are on the Red Rock Lakes refuge and should you visit this remote valley your chances of seeing trumpeters are excellent. By the unpaved road going east out of Monida toward West Yellowstone, it is twenty miles to refuge headquarters. There are also a few trumpeters in the potholes around Jackson Lake Lodge in Grand Teton National Park. And not far to the south are a few more pairs on the National Elk Refuge, where they are often hidden in the bulrushes and not easily seen from the highway. In Yellowstone National Park there are still trumpeters living on their historic nesting areas, on Swan Lake and Twin Lake and along the Madison River.

Once they had the swan numbers building again on Red Rock Lakes, the refuge workers began searching for logical places to reintroduce the trumpeters. Spreading them out would further help insure the safety of this species. In 1938 four cygnets were captured in late summer at Red Rock Lakes and turned loose in the Jackson Hole marshes. Through the following years others were moved to Malheur National Wildlife Refuge in southeastern Oregon, Ruby Lake National Wildlife Refuge in Nevada, and eventually even to South Dakota. There, twenty-two years after cygnets were first removed from Red Rock, two pairs were turned loose in Lacreek National Wildlife Refuge.

And there, in the summer of 1963, these transplanted trumpeters hatched four cygnets, the first trumpeters to hatch east of the Rockies and south of the Canadian border in more than eighty years!

The trumpeter swan has come back.

*Close Call for the
Littlest Deer*

Key Deer National Wildlife Refuge

12

Along the sun-washed string of islands stretching westward from Florida's mainland live the survivors of a tiny race of whitetail deer. The key deer, miniature copies of their larger cousins to the north, stand scarcely taller than a coon hound. The average buck weighs less than eighty pounds and measures twenty-eight inches at the shoulders.

The islands on which they live were once remote and isolated patches of tropical wilderness. But now the world of the key deer has jazz bands to harmonize with the lapping waves, neon lights to rival the stars, restaurants in the palmettos, and people everywhere. How the elusive little key deer staged a comeback so near civilization's syncopated beat is one of the more incredible wildlife stories of the age.

As far as anyone knows this race of deer has never lived anywhere else except in those islands of the lower Florida Keys which are underlaid, not with marl, but with oolitic limestone. Some have speculated that one reason may be the little reservoirs of fresh water held by the limestone in some places the year around.

To say how many deer lived on the keys in prehistoric times would be to speculate, for there is little evidence to tell us. Through the centuries they withstood tropical hurricanes, snakes, insects and shortages of fresh water. But poachers and bulldozers were more than they could cope

with. The poachers drove deer off the outlying keys into
the water to kill them. Sometimes they used hounds to
drive the deer out. On other occasions they used fire. In
either case the deer, once driven into the water, could not
turn back. The poacher waiting in his boat did not even
need a gun; he hit the animal in the head with a hatchet
and dragged it into his boat.

In later years came the hazard of the new highway
across the keys, as well as the accelerated development of
the keys as a vacation attraction for growing numbers of
people.

The eradication of the key deer might have been complete by now had it not been for a series of events beginning in 1937 in Atlanta, Georgia, seven hundred miles
to the north. That year, Jim Silver, a rodent-control and
predator expert with the Bureau of Biological Survey, became the Bureau's regional director for the Southeastern
states.

Meanwhile there had been a bustling industry in the
illegal trapping and sale of migratory songbirds. Silver dis-
patched patrolman Earle Greene to clean up the songbird
operations. In one of his earliest reports Greene sent word
to Silver in regional headquarters back in Atlanta that the
key deer were in serious trouble. The uninhabited islands
were being burned. And Silver soon found to his surprise
that his immediate problem was to protect the key deer
from the United States government.

"The burning," he told me, "was being done by employees of the Department of Agriculture. The boys on the
job had been instructed to eradicate the wild or tree cotton
which was prevalent on the key-deer range." Eradication
of the perennial cotton as a disease-host plant was thought
to be essential, and burning was the most efficient method.

"I doubt," said Silver, "that the department heads knew
anything about the burning." Silver promptly sent a letter
to the Washington office and the official burning ceased
abruptly. "But unfortunately," adds Silver, "the meat
hunters had learned how effective it was to chase the deer

off their island habitat with fire. There is little doubt that the cotton-eradication campaign gave impetus to the method.

"It was this investigation," Silver told me, "that made me realize what a precarious position the key deer were in. They needed help or their days were surely numbered."

Silver could also see that they were going to need more than local help. Across the keys, in fact, were real-estate developers ready to fight any move to set aside land for saving the deer.

How many deer were left? In 1947 Silver asked the question of Gerald F. Baker, who was in charge of all south Florida national wildlife refuges. The best figure they could arrive at was seventy. Once there had been seventy passenger pigeons left in the world, another time seventy heath hens.

Time was running out for the key deer, but Silver, responsible primarily for migratory waterfowl, had no authority and no funds for deer-refuge work. He decided that people outside Florida would care about what was happening if they knew the story. So he began writing a series of reports. The first one, dated January 27, 1950, was called "Memorandum to the Friends of Vanishing Wildlife." He sent copies to all the outdoor-minded people he could think of, leaders of conservation organizations, magazine and newspaper writers, anyone who might help spread the word.

"On a small group of subtropical keys, nearly one hundred miles south of the mainland of Florida," he wrote, "a small nucleus of the most unique deer in the United States is still hanging on to a precarious existence. These are the key deer, the smallest of all deer of the United States. Their numbers have been reduced to a possible 25 head but certainly no more than 50. In 1947," he added, "their numbers were estimated at 70 and further back they were much more numerous. . . . Formerly it ranged over much of the keys, from Key Largo to Key West, but due to the onward march of winter vacationists and land speculators much of their former range has been engulfed. The deer are now making a last ditch stand on Big Pine Key and a few adjacent islands."

He had now stated the problem and to this he added a solemn warning. "The tide of tourists and accompanying development of this remaining area is imminent," he said, "and once a start is made in cutting it up into town lots the few remaining deer will surely be crowded into the sea and lost forever."

Somehow, Silver said, land had to be acquired and set aside for the deer. Jim Silver figured the key deer range at no more than ten thousand acres. "Outright ownership and permanent setting aside of the 10,000 acres involved," he wrote, "for exclusive use of the deer is a minimum premise on which the salvation of the deer must depend." While this aim was laudatory from the point of view of a professional wildlife worker, it was hardly realistic in view of the rocketing land values in the Florida Keys.

From the first time Silver rang the alarm, people responded. By August of 1950 he had issued a progress report. "The plight of these toy deer," he announced, "has stirred the imagination and tugged strongly at the heart strings of a great many people."

One frequent suggestion was that the problem be solved by live-trapping key deer and moving them to areas already owned by the federal government. "This suggestion, however," said Silver, "is unthinkable, except as a last resort." The key deer, said the ecologists, would be hopelessly unable to cope with the pressures of a strange environment. "They would soon lose their identity," Silver predicted, "and be lost as a unique species almost as certainly as if they were permitted to perish in their natural environment."

What is the subtropical world of the key deer like? The islands on which they live are low; none is more than a few feet above sea level. At the very level of the sea, their roots in the tidewaters, are tangles of red and black mangrove rimming the islands. At slightly higher elevations there are the white mangroves, or buttonbush, mixed with the scrub palmetto, sea grape, pigeon plum, red bay, poisonwood and the gumbo limbo.

On the larger keys such as Big Pine, there are stands of slash pine and the thatch or silver palms so important to the deer. Then there are orchids and air plants adding brilliant tropical colors and rich variety to the jungle landscape. These islands are a delight for botanists. On Big Pine Key alone they have identified 390 species of plants.

There are rare and colorful birds to fit the setting. Here one may encounter the roseate spoonbill, the rare great white heron, the reddish egret, the gray kingbird and the big white-crowned pigeons. There are also the alligators and even a few of the now rare American crocodiles. The raccoon is abundant here but he is a pale variety that has almost lost the rings on his tail.

Over a four-year period Jim Silver wrote and distributed five of his progress reports. In the second of them he was able to report the first positive results.

In Washington one of the staunch friends of the key deer, Congressman Charles E. Bennett of Jacksonville, Florida, had introduced House Bill 7524 to authorize buying lands within the deer's range. The cost was estimated at $300,000, a figure which the committee considering the bill felt was too high. Then Fish and Wildlife Service technicians began paring down the acreage and the dollar figures in hopes of salvaging the bill.

At this point someone suggested leasing lands. These could be protected from fire and poachers and thus benefit the landowners as well as the animals. The landowner could terminate the lease anytime he wanted to, but here at least was temporary protection.

Some people asked meanwhile whether or not all this effort and expense in behalf of a few small deer was practical. Of course it was not practical. But who can judge by the calculations of a cash register what is lost when a species disappears from the face of the earth? Jim Silver admitted that the filling stations, eating places and fishing camps were vital and important parts of the American scene. "But so is the wildlife," he argued, "and there is room and need for both."

Silver's messages had aroused support across the country. The key deer would almost certainly never be listed again as legal game, but hunters quickly joined others in its support. The Boone and Crockett Club, a national organization of trophy hunters, donated the salary and expense money to hire a patrolman for one year.

They hired for the job Gerald Baker's assistant, Jack Watson, a cigar-smoking giant of a man with a near-religious fervor to protect the little deer. He went on the job May 26, 1951, and was shortly known up and down the keys as "the federal game warden."

Poaching dropped off quickly, fires seemed to start less frequently along the keys, and free-running dogs found themselves chained in their owners' yards for the first time in their lives.

When the Boone and Crockett funds ran out, the National Wildlife Federation was ready with money to enable Jack to continue working with the key deer.

Then in 1954, the Department of the Interior Appropriation Bill contained a clause enabling the Fish and Wildlife Service to manage lands within the natural habitat of the key deer. While there was still no way for the federal government to purchase these lands, Jim Silver's men could at least patrol against fire and poachers as part of their work. They could also lease lands and begin to construct water holes which might help keep the deer away from the lethal automobile and truck traffic which had been taking a growing toll of them on the U. S. highway to Key West. What still concerned conservationists was the fact that landowners could cancel out at any time they pleased. And sooner or later the real-estate values would make the temptation too much to resist.

Jack Watson had been on the job a year before he even saw his first key deer. "When we started in," he told me, "it was hard to even find a track." Then, however, he began to see the little deer with increasing frequency, and sometimes he saw two dozen in a week's time. The deer have spread out again to eighteen of their ancestral islands, and eventually there were several hundred of them.

The key deer, Watson learned, is exceptionally well fitted to his semi-aquatic existence. "They are excellent swimmers," he said. "They commonly swim from one key to the other. One day I found one swimming from No Name Key to Porpoise Key. I was in a sixteen-foot flat-bottom boat with a five-horse motor and the deer almost out-swam me. When I finally overtook him I wrestled him into the boat thinking I would take his measurements."

The buck had sizable antlers for a small animal and, as Watson recalled, once it was in the boat seemed to have more than four feet. The animal kicked up such a ruckus for his sixty or so pounds that Watson, in spite of the fact that he outweighed the deer by 150 pounds, quickly dumped the little buck back into the ocean.

"Another time," he said, "I found one mired down. I lassoed him and snubbed him to a tree. He made such a fuss I had to cut him loose. I'll never lasso another one."

When I talked with Watson, the federal government had seven thousand acres under lease at a dollar an acre per year, on a year-to-year basis. He had posted five hundred refuge signs around the borders of these areas.

Living, as he had for many years, right in the major population of key deer, Jack Watson had acquired considerable knowledge of their habits. "The rut," he said, "begins in February. Before that they spend a three months' period polishing their antlers."

Watson's carefully kept notes record the deer killed or seen along the highway. "Heaviest losses come in February, March and April." This is the period of the rut and the bucks are traveling just as bucks will in most regions.

Not every key deer that collides with a car, however, ends up a fatality. Watson told of one that ran into the side of a compact car and suffered nothing worse than a bloody nose. The car, however, was demolished. "The compact deer," said Watson, "made out better than the compact car."

Protection for the deer was the most pressing need. But the wildlife managers also wanted to accumulate more knowledge of how these animals lived. There had, for example, never been much learned about what they ate. A major food was found to be the red mangrove, *Rhizophora mangle,* almost as rich in protein as high-quality alfalfa. One thing seemed evident; there was no shortage of deer food on the keys.

In November of 1963, when the Key Deer National Wildlife Refuge was formally dedicated, it covered 6846 acres, but only 834 acres were owned outright by the Fish and Wildlife Service. Of this, 72 acres had come out of the public domain. Another 239 acres had been purchased by the Fish and Wildlife Service as part of the 1000 acres authorized by Congress. And another 523 acres had been bought by conservation-minded individuals and organizations with donations totaling $160,000, and turned over to the government. Future efforts will probably add more acreage to the land set aside permanently for the key deer.

Conservationists cross their fingers and hope that, at last, our littlest deer has been rescued for all time.

Saving Our Fastest Runner

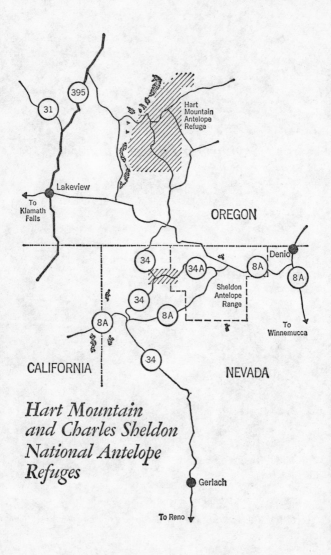

Hart Mountain
and Charles Sheldon
National Antelope
Refuges

13

Alert and tense, the buck antelope lifted his head above the sagebrush and scanned the countryside as far as he could see. For one brief moment he stood on the knoll in bold relief against the deep-blue autumn sky.

Then his head, carrying its fine set of short pronged horns, swung abruptly toward the east. Some distant flash of color or hint of motion had drawn his attention. In that instant the white hair on his rump stood erect to form a great white fan visible far across the prairies. Now he did not hesitate. His sharp hoofs were pounding the sand as he flashed through the powdery gray-green sagebrush, not dashing erratically here and there, but traveling in a line straight and true.

A dozen other antelope had joined him now and they were lined out in formation, all running at about the same speed. The buck struck his course parallel to the ranch lane, and the pickup truck, which had first attracted his attention while still four miles away, was gaining on him. The antelope knew now that the race was on. But still he did not travel at top speed.

Inside the truck the rancher, who never tired of watching the little band of antelope, glanced at his speedometer. Thirty-five, he thought, not bad, and he put more pressure on the accelerator while clouds of dust flew up from behind his truck. At forty-five he held his speed steady and the antelope stayed abreast. Then faster and faster they ran, gaining now on the truck, until, in one magnificent burst of speed they passed the truck, turned sharply and dashed across in front of it.

The antelope has a cruising speed of thirty-five or forty miles an hour, has little trouble getting up to fifty, and in a real race can hit bursts of sixty miles an hour—a mile a minute. The antelope seems to like the wind in his face.

This ability to run has helped keep him alive in the face of his natural enemies. But speed is not the only helpful characteristic the antelope has. Because his legs are almost as long as those of a cow, he can lift his head well above the sage and grasses on which he lives, and scan the prairies for signs of coyotes or wolves. And his eyes, by most standards, are out of all proportion to the size of his body. They measure an inch and a half in diameter and are as big as the eyes of a horse weighing many times as much.

An antelope has heart. He has a heart twice as big as that of sheep of equal weight, and a windpipe twice the size of a man's. So great are his oxygen requirements that he breathes through his open mouth from the moment he begins to run.

Most Western fences, except the sheep fences, do not turn antelope. Unlike the deer or elk, the average pronghorn apparently never thinks of going over the top of a fence that he can go through. An antelope can wiggle through or beneath a fence at top speed. At forty miles an hour he may hardly slow his pace as he hits the wires. And patches of his loose hair hang on the barbed wires behind him to mark his passage. In spite of this recklessness, surprisingly few antelope are ever seriously injured on fences.

The antelope's peculiar horns have long been an item of curiosity among men. Some have said antelope shed their horns each year, while others insist that they never shed them. The difference lies somewhere between; they do a little of both. Actually, the antelope is the only animal in the world that sheds just the sheath, the outer covering, of its horns. It retains the core of the horn and on this a new sheath forms quickly after the old one drops off. The sheath is formed of mats of hair-like fibers. It loosens and falls off in autumn after the breeding season and is soon consumed by rodents that discover it on the plains.

The doe's horns are a scant two to three inches in length, but the buck, especially an old solitary animal, may have horns eight or ten inches long. A set of twelve- or thirteen-inch horns is trophy size.

Speed, horns, exceptional hearing, sight and sense of smell, the antelope has them all. He also has a peculiar type of hair to give him his own air-conditioning system. In fall he sheds his finer coat of hair and acquires a covering of coarse hollow hairs, each of which is filled with air cells. Engineers have long known that dead air is among the most efficient insulators. They have employed the principle in the construction of many things, including sleeping bags, in which fillings of fluffy materials lock in air much as the down of a goose protects it from cold. Each individual hair of the antelope has its air cells. But in addition, the animal, by muscular control, can make its hair lie flat in overlapping layers or stand erect, permitting circulation of air through it.

The hair on the rump of the antelope, almost white and three inches long, has a special job. When the animal is startled, these two patches of hair on his posterior stand erect and flash into a white fan that flags the message to others of his kind all across the prairies. And other antelope for miles around accept the truth of the message without question and they in turn pass it on. Shortly all the antelope in sight may be off at top speed to escape a danger which most of them may not have seen. Automatically, as he signals danger with his rump fan, the antelope releases a strong scent from musk glands. And even a sleeping antelope can be awakened and set in motion by this startling odor.

In May, as the plains turn green, does begin to leave the bands with which they have roamed and search out nearby places to drop their fawns. If it is the doe's first fawn, there will likely be a single birth. In later years she almost invariably has twins.

For the first week of their lives the young lie hidden among the sagebrush, motionless for long periods of time, their bodies flattened against the earth and their long ears lying back against their necks. At this age a young antelope, like the fawn of a deer, is almost odorless. But should an enemy come too close after the fawn is ten days to two weeks old, he bounds to his feet and dashes off at speeds of twenty-five miles an hour. Within a week or two after giving birth the doe takes her fawns and rejoins her band, where the young romp together and the older animals nurse them and stand guard.

Meanwhile, the old bucks, often fat and inactive, will be off by themselves, where sometimes you see them standing majestically on a slight rise or knoll surveying the plains. These, incidentally, are often the trophy animals for which the serious hunter is willing to watch and stalk for days.

The life of an antelope, by many standards, is not a long one. At one and a half years they have reached breeding age and in perhaps three years more they live out their lives.

Here is an all-American animal, a native, not an immigrant like the deer and the bear which wandered to these shores in what must, in any geological reckoning, be considered recent times. The pronghorn is the only remaining member of his family, and is not a true antelope. Nowhere else in the world is there an animal that closely resembles him.

As the supreme predator, man hunted the antelope relentlessly—for many decades without control and without serious thought of saving enough to replenish the stock he was decimating. Consequently, antelope numbers were reduced to a point where extinction seemed assured. An animal whose family had hung on through twenty million precarious years was almost wiped out by man in half a century.

Perhaps there were fewer antelope than some early explorers thought. Some placed the number at sixty million and even one hundred million. But at best these were estimated by people largely untrained in counting wildlife populations. Some wildlife specialists now doubt that antelope were so abundant.

The antelope provided meat for the earliest explorers, the military, the train crews and the homesteaders. These settlers brought livestock, fences and plows and began to change the character of the West. The bands of antelope were still there, but their numbers were dwindling, and by the late 1800s Westerners saw fewer and fewer of them.

In 1908 the best available estimate of their remaining numbers was offered by Dr. T. S. Palmer, who felt that there were a scant twenty thousand pronghorns remaining north of Mexico. Others considered this estimate too liberal. At that time there were also still a few thousand in Mexico. So there may have been scarcely more than twenty thousand in the world at the time.

Rancher Perry Wallace, in some of the best antelope country in the West, told me that when he homesteaded east of Gillette, Wyoming, in 1916, he almost never saw an antelope. And Andy Forsythe, who began ranching in the Centennial Valley of southwestern Montana in what is excellent antelope country today, told me the antelope were extreme rarities when he arrived.

With the close call of the buffalo still fresh in their memories, people across the country were asking what, if anything, might now be done for the hard-pressed antelope. Among those Western states most determined to do something to aid the pronghorn was Oregon, where the antelope had now been reduced to remnant herds, most of which were in the southeastern part of the state around Hart Mountain and northward around Malheur Lake.

In what was probably the most accurate account of Oregon's antelope to that time, investigator Stanley G. Jewett concluded in 1915 that, in all of Oregon, there were 1840 pronghorns. Long-range scientific investigation of the Oregon antelope herds had its beginning, however, in 1936, when the Oregon Cooperative Wildlife Research Unit was established at Corvallis. This was one of the first in a new program to set up university training and research centers for wildlife-management specialists. The unit leader, Arthur S. Einarsen, began detailed field studies of the antelope, which by that time in Oregon was classed as a problem species because of its scarcity.

The same year the Oregon research project was launched, another positive effort in the fight to save the antelope was being made on Hart Mountain. And this was the end result of a campaign begun years earlier by E. R. Sans, a long-time worker for the U. S. Biological Survey.

Sans was carrying on an effort that, years earlier, had proved unsuccessful. From 1922 to 1924 agencies of the federal government and the sixteen states where antelope still remained had cooperated on a census of the remaining pronghorns. "Almost throughout its range," the report concluded, "the pronghorn is decreasing. Each succeeding year some of the smaller bands are certain to disappear." Consequently, Edward W. Nelson, chief of the U. S. Bureau of Biological Survey, called for a combined meeting of all those agencies concerned with perpetuating the antelope. From all over the country they assembled in the auditorium of the new Natural History Museum in Washington, D.C., on December 14, 1923. Charles Sheldon was there for the Boone and Crockett Club, T. Gilbert Pearson for the National Audubon Society, and Will Dilg for the Izaak Walton League. There were representatives of almost every major conservation organization of the day, plus senators and the director of the National Park Service. During the afternoon a committee met and drew up a bill for a proposed refuge for antelope, and also sage hens, in southeastern Oregon. But years were to pass before the antelope would get this protection.

Sans was concerned about the remnant bands of antelope, gun shy and harassed, on dry lake beds and deserts of northern Nevada and south-central Oregon. It had been his dream for years that the long-advocated refuge might be established there, perhaps in the vicinity of the Last Chance Ranch, in time to save the pronghorns.

But he made little progress until one day in 1928 he learned that Dr. T. Gilbert Pearson, president of the National Audubon Society, was coming to the West. Dr. Pearson's real interest was a nesting colony of white pelicans, but he also went with Sans to see the antelope range, and he understood then the merits of Sans's inspiration. Now Sans had an influential voice on his side.

Back in New York, having visited both the pelicans and the antelope, Dr. Pearson began talking of the antelope refuge with members of the Boone and Crockett Club, of which he was a member. That autumn up in Nova Scotia, Charles Sheldon, a robust and vigorous outdoorsman, friend of Teddy Roosevelt and long a member of the Boone and Crockett Club, died of a sudden heart attack. Other members of the Boone and Crockett Club were in a mood to establish a monument to Sheldon's memory. He had hunted through the West and the antelope had been one of his favorite animals.

The National Audubon Society and the Boone and Crockett Club raised $10,000 each and with this they purchased 119 acres of privately owned land in the heart of the Last Chance Ranch country. They promptly turned this over to the federal government as the required nucleus of a national antelope refuge.

On January 26, 1931, Sans saw his dream become reality when President Hoover, by executive order, created the Sheldon National Antelope Refuge. He had added enough public land to the original gift to make a total of more than thirty-four thousand acres. Sans, however, had studied antelope long enough to realize that this single area was probably not enough to guarantee their safety. He knew they traveled with the seasons, and that three states, Nevada, Oregon and California, shared the same antelope.

Not many years later, Oregon people, including Dr. Ira N. Gabrielson, who was then doing field work in that state for the Bureau of Biological Survey, were advocating another antelope refuge in the Hart Mountain section of that state. President Franklin D. Roosevelt's executive order creating the Hart Mountain National Antelope Refuge came in 1936. And, at the same time, he enlarged the Sheldon National Antelope Refuge by adding to it 549,000 acres of adjacent lands which became the Charles Sheldon Antelope Range. Sans was transferred there as superintendent, and he stayed until his retirement in 1942.

Now the remnant herd had protection the year around. Straight across the open desert country it is about twenty miles from Hart Mountain to Sheldon. Antelope make the trip depending on the seasons. The high, cool slopes of Hart Mountain provide a favorite fawning area for them. But here winters are harsh and food often unavailable, so they drift down to lower regions. They cross over into Nevada to the Sheldon National Antelope Refuge for the winter.

Once the Hart-Sheldon refuges were established, the antelope began a gradual increase in numbers. About two thousand antelope now live in these refuges.

Hart Mountain, which rises 8020 feet above sea level, was the product of a volcano. Separating the mountain plateau from the floor of Warner Valley are spectacular rugged cliffs. Down the face of the cliffs several streams have cut spectacular canyons, among them Hart, Potter, and the wild and rugged DeGarmo Canyon. In Warner Valley, which holds the potential of becoming one of the Pacific Flyway's finest waterfowl refuges, a whole series of shallow lakes, including Hart, Anderson, Stone Corral and Bluejoint, lie at the foot of the Hart Mountain escarpment.

On its east slope Hart Mountain drops away more gently. Numerous springs scattered over the mountain area provide water for wildlife. Its life zones, ranging from the semi-desert of the Upper Sonoran zone to the Canadian zones found in its cool canyons, give this refuge area a wide variety of plants and animals. Here the mountain sheep once roamed. They were common on Hart Mountain until 1890. In 1954 the Fish and Wildlife Service and the Oregon State Game Commission obtained twenty mountain sheep from British Columbia and brought them down to Hart Mountain.

At the site of an old army post, high up in the transition zone at about 6600 feet, is a fine stand of Western yellow, or ponderosa, pine. Bird watchers come here to see the mountain chickadee, red-breasted nuthatch, evening grosbeak, red crossbill, and even Steller's jay. The Hart Mountain bird list, including species observed down in the lake country of Warner Valley, includes 225 species.

On Sheldon National Antelope Refuge tree growth, except for juniper and mountain mahogany, is sparse. This is high country with semi-desert tablelands and mesas cut up by lava-walled canyons. In elevation it ranges from 4500 to 7600 feet above sea level. Summers here are warm and winters usually marked by blizzards and deep snows. The antelope share the country with mule deer as well as some coyotes, jackrabbits and bobcats. The bird list totals 147 species. Much of this vast range is remote, isolated and seldom visited by outsiders.

In Oregon, as elsewhere throughout the antelope range, the pronghorn antelope has been granted a reprieve. They have come back in such numbers that hunting seasons are annual affairs in several Western states.

This, of course, has its built-in hazards too. Casual observers, and in this group we must include most hunters, still tend to overestimate the numbers of antelope. Accepting their own guesses as fact, they are then quick to demand more liberal hunting seasons. And history tells us that the biggest threat facing the antelope is heavy hunting pressure.

What does tomorrow hold for the antelope? Is he really secure now from the shadow of extinction that stalked him at the turn of the century? A hint at the answer may lie in the past. This, at least, is what Oscar Deming, formerly a refuge biologist, believed. He traced the vicissitudes of the pronghorn back, as he said "almost to year one." And he has gathered from history an understanding of the animal's needs and an uneasiness about its future.

"We talk a lot about antelope range," he said, "but just what is antelope range? The antelope range we see antelope living on now is the sage, forbs, grass-plant community but this doesn't mean they have always lived in such a plant community or that this is the best habitat for them."

Deming, as I soon discovered, viewed the antelope as a product of climate. "It was not until the Miocene period, about twenty million years ago," he told a group of his fellow workers at a wildlife conference, "that the surface of the earth assumed a vegetation cover that was suitable for the development of grazing plains animals. The Miocene is known for the rapid spreading of the grasses that had so long been sub-dominant under the overhanging canopy of vast and old subtropical forests. The cooler drier climate of the Miocene was the stimulus needed to open up these old forests and spread the grasses to form vast prairies, plains and veldts. From the first harsh, stubby blades of green grass there evolved, in time, the forage plants and cereals that we know today.

"By the end of the Miocene period the open, sun-drenched plains were teeming with an abundance of grazing animals, the like of which has never been equalled. But the climate was cooling, and in the north the ice caps were beginning to form."

The colder climate brought to the Southwest hardier grasses that replaced the tall grass of the prairies. Deserts replaced the subtropical forests of that region. Then the great ice sheets pushed farther and farther southward, bringing freezing temperatures to a third of the earth. Eventually grasslands returned to the West, but now the sagebrush was there too, a product of the dry climate.

This, in itself, was never bad for the antelope. The sagebrush pushed northward behind the retreating glaciers and mixed with the grasses. Then into this scene marches the white man with his domesticated livestock, which proceeded to overgraze the range.

This came at a time in history, according to Deming's studies, particularly bad for the antelope. The country was by then in the grip of a long-term drought which, combined with heavy grazing, reduced the grasses and let the sage become dominant. Today, antelope are living, not always well, on territory predominantly sagebrush. Consequently men in some areas have come to think of sage and antelope together and assume that the thicker the sage the better off the antelope. But, as Deming has pointed out, antelope do better where they have a mixture of grasses, forbs and sage.

"It is my belief," he says, "that we are now living in a time of crisis for the antelope. The pronghorn antelope, born in a day of lush grasslands, endured the changes made upon the face of the earth as the glaciers advanced and retreated and is persisting today on ranges that bear little resemblance to its historic one. I am of the opinion that the antelope is close to the limits to which it can change and endure, and continued changes in climate and habitat could result in the extermination of the antelope."

Here then, wildlife specialists are trying to save an animal that is living under conditions far different from those it faced when it developed on this part of the earth twenty million years ago. Men have saved the antelope, at least for the present, in spite of the fact that it may not even have history in its favor. For any creature living close to the limits of its tolerance, the smallest change can mean disaster.

Three Arch Rocks

Three Arch Rocks
National Wildlife Refuge

14

Scarcely a mile out in the Pacific, opposite the village of Oceanside, Oregon, are three black, inhospitable-looking rocks rising in forbidding cliffs from the turbulent sea. This little cluster of islands is the stage for a great bird drama that begins each year on a night in May.

On this night, from far out at sea, great flocks of heavy-bodied, stubby-winged murres descend on the islands. Guided by some system still not understood by men, they fly with uncanny accuracy toward land until the dark shapes of the three little islands loom up before them almost at the ocean's edge. The murres, as if not quite willing to give up their freedom for the weeks of domestic responsibility ahead, may wheel and go back toward the sea. But they return and crowd in to claim their own fraction of this famous wildlife refuge.

Half a million fish-eating birds come to the seventeen-acre Three Arch Rocks National Wildlife Refuge in June and July to raise their young. Here, just beyond convenient binocular range of the Oregon coast, is one of the nation's outstanding bird spectacles. Living with the murres are the petrels, gulls, cormorants, kittiwakes and, the clowns among them, tufted puffins.

The Three Arch Rocks refuge is one of many such bird rocks along the coast from San Francisco Bay to the Aleutians, several of them now protected as national wildlife refuges. A visit here can be an unforgettable experience, as Bob Twist assured me when I first met him. "Any time you want to go to Three Arch Rocks," he said, "I'm ready. That's the noisiest place I've ever been," he added, "but the most exciting."

Twist, a graduate forester and a refuge manager for the Fish and Wildlife Service, was talking so fast now in his excitement that his words tumbled over each other. "When you climb up on those islands," he said, "you know you are one of the few men ever to stand there. And the wildlife all around you is living just the way it was centuries ago. The Three Arch Rocks refuge," and there was a note of awe in his voice, "is one of the few places man has not plowed, burned, drained or covered with concrete. That's a wonderful place for anyone interested in wildlife."

As you approach the islands you can see that the tops, as well as the north-facing slopes, a total perhaps of two acres, are covered with a sparse growth of surf grass. The Three Arch Rocks have withstood the pounding surf for countless ages. But the sea has left its mark. It has, in fact, carved tunnels completely through each of the three islands at water level to form the arches from which the islands get their name.

So important are these islands to the nesting birds that anyone going onto them must first have permission from the refuge headquarters, which is in the Willapa National Wildlife Refuge at Ilwaco, Washington. The simple physical act of going ashore on the Three Arch Rocks can be highly dangerous. One must plan carefully, and have luck on his side as well, to keep the breakers from rolling him into the sea with all his equipment. "I have only been on the outer island," Twist told me. "There is only one place on the island to get ashore."

Twist, at the time, was refuge manager of the Willapa National Wildlife Refuge. And as far as he knew no other refuge manager had ever gone ashore on the Three Arch Rocks, even to post the islands with the famous sign of the flying goose. Lured by the promise of seeing the nesting activities of the sea birds close at hand, Twist had visited the area three times.

First he found a fishing-boat captain who knew the region. He had the mother ship take him to within 150 yards of the outer rock, which was as close as the captain cared to venture. They had waited for the favorable north wind and a low tide, and the breakers, even then, were five feet high. Twist sat in the bow of a rowboat and had one of his companions row it close to the island. They studied the procession of waves crashing against the rocks and breaking into fogs of spray. At the right moment they maneuvered the boat onto one of the waves and rode the crest of it up to the rocks.

As each wave peaked, it hesitated for a scant fifteen seconds, "just long enough," Twist said, "to jump out of the boat and get onto the rocks." The rocks are normally crumbly, and seaweeds and salt spray make them slippery. Twist scrambled up on a shelf knowing that if he should slip there would be little his friend could do to help him out of the water.

Meanwhile the oarsman was rowing as fast as he could to pull away from the island before the next waves could bring him crashing back against the rocks. Later he returned with a second member of the crew and fought to hold the boat off while supplies were tossed to Twist. There were sleeping bags and food for an overnight stay and also two signs, complete with steel posts. There were even two bags of cement which they managed to get ashore successfully.

Now, for the first time, Twist was a part of this busy, noisy offshore domain of birds and sea lions.

The murres seemed to be everywhere. How many were there? The populations can change from year to year, but Twist, with pilot-biologist Ray Glahn, of the Fish and Wildlife Service, had flown over the islands to make aerial photographs on which they could actually count the birds. On the seventeen acres, they had photographed 320,000 murres, almost a third of a million! Twist found when he visited the islands that "The murres crowd every available inch. They even nest in arches in the semi-darkness." They are, in many ways, a most remarkable bird.

The murres are the most abundant nesting birds in the coastal bird colonies. Almost certainly, available nesting space is a factor that limits their numbers, and at this critical period in their year the refuge bird rocks are their best guarantee of safety.

Like immaculately clad, seventeen-inch deacons, the murres stand on their rock ledges. Their underparts are white, their heads, wings and backs a dark rich brown. Their feet are webbed and their legs are placed penguin style so far back on their bodies that murres stand almost on end. Row on row they line the ledges, up the island and over the top, crowding the slopes until it looks like the multitude assembled for the Sermon on the Mount.

There was a time when the biggest known hazard to these birds, and other pelagic sea birds, were the human poachers who collected their eggs to sell in city markets. These wild eggs were delicacies in San Francisco, and consequently the bird islands off the coast of California were heavily preyed upon. Even after laws made such egg collecting illegal, the trade went on. In the six years following 1850 there were, according to old records, between three and four million sea-bird eggs sold in San Francisco.

The murres do little to affect man's daily life. They do not eat grasshoppers as do the gulls, mess up sidewalks, feed on tender sweet corn or consume carpenter ants. They're just out there, as they have been for hundreds of centuries, neither bothering anyone particularly nor providing men with much practical reason for spending money and effort in their behalf. But the world would be a little duller without them, as it would be without the whooping crane.

Murres, as one might suspect, live largely on fish. The sea is their great dependable pantry. They rely on the small fish, mullet being a favorite. They sometimes capture mullet much as the plains Indians once hunted buffalo; they stage a "surround." The submerged murres ride herd on a school of mullet and quickly overtake and dispatch any fish that becomes frantic and tries to break away, a practice almost certainly more efficient than darting into the middle of the school and scattering fish in every direction. Underwater the murre is in his element. He uses both his wings and his feet and goes with such speed that he can outswim the fish on which he feeds.

The murres court and mate while still en route to the Three Arch Rocks. The female lays one egg. Perhaps this is just as well because, built as she is, caring for even one egg becomes a full-time task. The murres build no nest. They simply place their treasure on a rock ledge, perhaps a hundred feet above the roaring surf and only inches from the edge of the cliff. To the human eye one spot on this ledge may look like any other spot. But the birds see a difference. They know which is their own nesting territory and somehow recognize it. Bird banding has shown that the pairs even return to their old position on the same ledge year after year to lay their eggs.

Naturalists noticed years ago a peculiar and fortunate fact about the egg of the murre; it comes to a sharper point on one end than the eggs of most birds. What's so good about this? With one large end and one small end the murre eggs do not roll like an ordinary hen's egg. Set in motion, the murre's egg is more likely to roll in tight little circles like a top and come to rest before it reaches the edge of the cliff. This must be credited more to evolution than planning, but whatever the explanation, murres should count the shape of their eggs among their blessings. Some murres, however, still lose their precious eggs in the shuffle. The young sea lions fancy them and the brash gulls steal them. And if the colony is suddenly disturbed, the scrambling parents kick some eggs off the ledges.

"The eggs have tough shells," Bob Twist said, "and they are irregularly splotched with darker colors." The patterns on them come in endless variations and it may be, as some ornithologists believe, that the parents looking out on this garden of eggs can pick out their own by its markings. The female entrusts the egg to her mate while she goes off to feed. At other times the male stands nearby.

When a murre returns from his fishing he makes a dead-stick landing in among his neighbors and jostles and crowds through them toward his mate. The other birds scold and push but serious fighting is rare.

A murre's wings are short and his body heavy, making it difficult for him to become airborne, especially on a calm day. To get into the air from the water, he runs along the surface and, where possible, takes off into the wind. Built as they are, murres cannot launch themselves directly into the air from their crowded rock ledges. Their alternative is simplicity itself; they just go to the edge of the cliff and jump over. As they fall toward the sea, they beat their stubby wings frantically and level off in a long graceful curve near the water. Once aloft they are fairly strong fliers. It is in their landings and take-offs that they could use some practice.

"If you scare them off the ledges," said Twist, "they make the awfullest noise you ever heard. They come tumbling down all around you, squawking, and calling and falling on each other in the water." If there are young in the colony, the old birds begin to return almost immediately and bedlam is the order of the day. The adults make their awkward landings and push and shove, inspecting each young bird they come to, rejecting and even pecking some with their sharp beaks until reunited with the one they somehow recognize.

The old birds have difficulty coaxing the young ones into the sea. One could hardly blame the chicks. They have no experience to tell them they can fly or that they are expert divers. They are, in fact, still half covered with soft down. Their only world has been within inches of the rocky bed where the egg was first deposited. Now somewhere down there on the rolling seas, in the darkness of night, their parents ask them to jump off a cliff. The reluctant chick hangs back calling for his parents to come to him instead. Then, too close to the edge, he loses his footing and his balance and goes tumbling into the Pacific, where the old birds promptly get him between them and swim off to sea, turning their backs on the Three Arch Rocks, and their view of Oceanside, Oregon, for another year.

The murres have for neighbors the tufted puffins, which seem more particular about their homes. The number of these strange-looking little birds nesting on the Three Arch Rocks may vary greatly from year to year. Aerial photographs made by Ray Glahn showed seventy-five or eighty living there.

Those who think it a disadvantage to be different should be glad they are not tufted puffins. This bird has a great high parrot-like beak with a grip like a snapping turtle and sharp cutting edges that can slice a man's hand to the bone. More than one person has had this forcibly demonstrated, because the tufted puffin is a scrappy individual with a strong sense of property rights.

The adult, which stands about fifteen inches high, changes its uniform with the seasons. Its winter colors are somber browns and blacks. But when the season for courtship and family living comes on, the puffin is as bright and colorful as a member of the home-town band. His beak, feet and eye rings are splashed with brilliant oranges. And on either side of his head is a four-inch tuft of straw-colored feathers that blow gaily in the stiff sea breeze as the bird stands guard at the entrance of the nesting cave. His tufts, however, as far as men have ever learned, have no more practical purpose than a necktie.

The puffins usually nest in a tunnel four or five feet long which they dig beneath the shallow topsoil that, in some places, caps the bird rocks. Here the female places a single egg. It is a thick-shelled, lusterless creation, but it is treated as carefully as if it were beautiful. While one of the parents incubates it, the mate assumes guard duty at the entrance of the cave.

Unlike the murres, the puffins do not coax or trick their

young into the sea. They have simplified this process. As if they had all the domesticity they can stand, they simply swim away from the island one day and abandon the young bird in the nest. For a week or so he lives off his fat. Then, perhaps driven by hunger, he waddles and tumbles off the face of the cliff and swims off to sea all alone.

The downstairs neighbors of all the birds on these small islands are the great massive sea lions. They haul themselves out of the ocean to loaf on the rocks just beyond reach of the roaring surf. Even the huge bulls, which may be twelve feet long and weigh nearly a ton, can clamber up the rocks on their flippers with amazing agility. The petite females, assembled twelve to fifteen to the harem, are considerably smaller.

When Bob Twist and Ray Glahn photographed these islands, they found a herd of three hundred sea lions summering there. These are the animals that move on southward in the winter and make room for other sea lions that come down from the Aleutians and the Pribilof Islands. The young, which weigh thirty-five to fifty pounds at birth and measure thirty-eight to forty inches long, are born shortly after the cows arrive on the islands in early May. Within a couple of months the young sea lions have doubled their weight and spend much of their time in the water.

In times past people found uses for nearly every part of the sea lion. The hides covered kayaks and the flesh became food. The fat was marketed as a lubricant, the intestines stitched into raincoats, and the whiskers sold in the Orient for cleaning the stems of opium pipes. There was even a market for the male's reproductive organs, which were dried, ground and sold in the Orient, where men believed they would restore youthful vitality.

Today there is still a breed of commercial fisherman who, believing that the sea lion feeds heavily on commercial fish, carries a 30-.06 in his boat. If he comes upon a sea lion while there is a fog to hide his crime, he turns his rifle on the creature in what he considers justifiable retribution. But these animals get more blame than they deserve. Investigators have found that much of their food is crustacea and small fish of no commercial value. Unhampered by such facts, men have harassed the sea lions until they have long since abandoned old haunts on the mainland. Today a large fraction of those remaining spend at least a part of their year on various national wildlife refuges such as Three Arch Rocks.

There they share the fishing waters with the sea birds and an occasional angler out for lingcod, or snapper. And they retire as they please behind the protection of the signs that Bob Twist erected, on what he still considers his most exciting adventure as a refuge manager.

Tule Lake

Tule Lake
and
Other National Wildlife Refuges

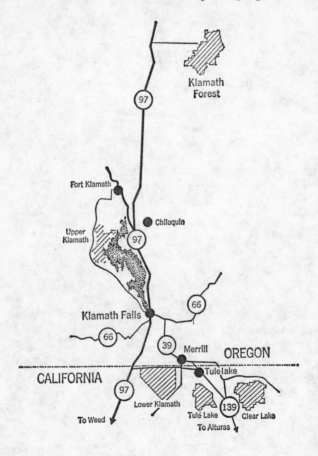

15

We read that our ancestors encountered waterfowl on this continent in numbers that stagger the imagination, that the roar of wings drowned conversation as ducks rose in clouds thick as plagues of locusts in biblical times. And we say as we read these accounts, if we believe them, that those days are history now and gone forever.

But take cheer, because I can tell you about a place where you will of an October day see a million ducks—or maybe five million.

The place is the Klamath Basin, which bridges the Oregon-California border within sight of Mount Shasta. Here, clustered within forty miles of the city of Klamath Falls, Oregon, are five national wildlife refuges, totaling 125,196 acres—Upper Klamath, Lower Klamath, Klamath Forest, Clear Lake, and Tule Lake. Best-known of the five is Tule Lake, the most important single waterfowl refuge in the country. Pintails, mallards, American widgeons, white-fronted geese, snow geese and cackling geese gather here in the greatest concentration of waterfowl anywhere on the continent and perhaps in the world.

Into this valley every fall come 80 percent of all the waterfowl migrating down the Pacific Flyway. Tule Lake is such a magnet that in October great flocks of ducks detour across the Cascades from the western edge of the flyway. Meanwhile, others turn west to come in from the Snake River in Idaho. From all parts of the fly-way they funnel into the fertile Klamath Valley, where their ancestors stopped in their southbound travels long before the white man walked here. Here is waterfowl hunting that may be the best left in the country today. No other refuge in the federal system has a public hunting area as large as this one. Nor does any other refuge farm twenty-five hundred acres to grow duck feed. Tule Lake National Wildlife Refuge even maintains a duck hospital with an outstanding success record.

The first refuge in this cluster of five was Lower Klamath National Wildlife Refuge, so far north in California that it borders Oregon. In 1908 the concentrations of waterfowl here prompted conservationists and ornithologists to urge President Theodore Roosevelt to turn the lake into a refuge. That year it became the first national refuge set aside for waterfowl.

Twenty-five miles to the east is Clear Lake, famed for the largest nesting colony of white pelicans in the United States. The big fish-eating birds nest here in the broad stands of round-stemmed bulrushes, or "tules." Clear Lake became a refuge in 1911 by presidential executive order.

Then in 1928 still other executive orders set aside two more refuges in the Klamath Basin. One was the Upper Klamath, north and west of the city of Klamath Falls. The other was Tule Lake. Now the complex of refuges in the basin was complete. But the future of the ducks and geese was far from secure. There has been a long history of competition, especially in the fertile lake-bottom lands of Tule Lake, between waterfowl and farmers. If you fly over Tule Lake today, you may see potato harvesters and pintails at the same time, combines and gadwalls, farm trucks and white-fronted geese.

This contest for space began almost with the first white man to cross the Cascades probing the wilderness riches. What did these explorers find in that million-acre valley? Marshes and broad, shallow lakes marked the landscape;

water covered more than 400,000 acres of the Klamath Basin.

No one knows how many ducks and geese passed down through this keyhole in the Pacific Flyway in those days. But the wealth of waterfowl soon attracted the market hunters. Records show that a single company, the San Francisco Game Transfer Company, in but one season late in the 1890s shipped from the Klamath Basin more than 120 tons of ducks. Close on the heels of the market hunters came the farmers. This century had hardly begun when they started draining the shallow marshes along the north edge of Tule Lake. The soils were black, deep and fertile. Here was a land of promise. Only one thing was wrong—water, not too little of it, even though the rainfall was a scant ten inches a year, but too much of it.

Shortly the federal government, searching for new areas in which to encourage homesteading, saw the promise in the black soils of Tule Lake. Oregon and California quickly agreed to turn over lands here to the federal government, and the Reclamation Service, predecessor of the Bureau of Reclamation, was on the scene officially by 1905.

As the acreages of water dwindled through the years, the ducks did not change their patterns of migration. They continued to come and crowd into the remaining wetlands. And they were in the farmers' grain fields consuming great quantities of barley. Next, the Klamath Basin pintails, hundreds of thousands strong, would depart the waters of Tule Lake and head for the bustling Sacramento Valley of central California. Here, in spite of all the noise the farmers could make, the ducks would feed on the ripening rice. Then, if the rice should give out, and perhaps even if it didn't, the waterfowl might once more head south, this time to stop over in the Imperial Valley in the southern part of the state. Here they would feast on the highly valued lettuce crops.

Through the years this has been the problem facing refuge managers. How could they keep great concentrations of waterfowl living in harmony with the concentrated agriculture of the irrigated valleys along the Pacific Flyway? The value of the farm crops to the human population could hardly be debated. But neither could the value of the ducks and geese.

The answer supplied by the refuge people at Tule Lake was to go into the farming business. Grow the good things the ducks like to eat, and keep them from moving on to crops not intended for their use. "Our big job," the refuge manager explained to me, "is to grow a quarter of a million bushels of barley a year, plus green crops for the geese. This way we can hold the waterfowl here much later in the season, and until crops are harvested in the rice fields down south. If the ducks were to move on south, they would also be vulnerable to more days of hunting during the season. If we weren't here," he added, "there would be a much reduced waterfowl population in the Pacific Flyway."

If this grain farming, part of which is done by sharecroppers, does not keep the twenty-two permanent workers on the five refuges busy, there are still signs, fences, roadways, buildings and drainage ditches to keep in repair.

A good portion of the seventy-five thousand visitors who come to the refuge each year find their way to the headquarters building five miles west of Tulelake, California. Most of them are sight-seeing, some are serious bird watchers and many come during the annual waterfowl hunting season, which is famous up and down the coast. Hunters begin arriving a couple of days before the season's opening. They camp in trucks, tents and trailers in rows along the gravel road that skirts the base of Sheepy Ridge west of the headquarters building. They scout the area, and many of them come in time to spend a couple of days deer hunting in the nearby national forests.

No hunting permits are required and there is no limit on the number who may hunt the refuge. For many years 28 percent of Tule Lake refuge and 21 percent of

Lower Klamath have been open during the waterfowl season. Duck hunters build their own blinds, which they must later remove. Or, more often, they simply hunt from rowboats which they push in among the tules, or bulrushes. They pull the vegetation down over themselves in a simple blind that hides them from passing ducks and geese.

And, from blind after blind, they come in with limits of both pintails and white-fronted geese. "Limits are the rule," the refuge manager told me, "on both ducks and geese." How do the hunters know which areas are open to them and which are closed? "We put up green signs on the public hunting areas," said the manager, "and red on the areas that are closed." When they have a special pheasant hunt, as they do most years, they mark these areas with yellow signs. In a recent ten-year period the Klamath Basin refuges logged an average of 24,577 hunters a year. They bagged an average of 40,688 ducks each year, and 18,542 geese. There are nine thousand acres open to waterfowl and fourteen thousand acres open to pheasant hunters.

Low water is enough to frighten a refuge manager at Tule Lake. "If we get a thin film of water over a mud flat," he explains, "we have more botulism because conditions are good for anaerobic bacteria. In alkaline water as the temperature rises the algae decomposes more rapidly and uses oxygen in the process and the botulinus organisms flourish. Then the ducks come along and feed on these mud flats and that's when we get sick ducks." So deadly is botulism to ducks that some years ago the refuge staff built a duck hospital especially to treat this food poisoning. Now as they go about their refuge duties in late summer they keep a sharp watch for sick ducks. And when botulism is serious they make daily trips out in air-boats to gather up the ailing waterfowl and bring them back to the duck hospital.

There they are inoculated with botulism antitoxin and left in crates with water and feed. As they regain their health and become more active, the ducks are transferred to an enclosure that is two hundred feet by forty feet, and which has a small pond in the center. Around this enclosure is a five-foot-high fence. When the ducks are well enough to clear the fence they return to the marshes and the barley fields under their own power. For some it is only an overnight stay in the hospital, but others may take three days to recover. Their disease is non-transmissible. "We have treated as many as eight thousand in a year," the refuge manager told me, "and we average five thousand." How many do they save? The recovery rate runs 90 percent, an average of forty-five hundred ducks a year saved, birds that without treatment would almost certainly die.

But while high water levels help control botulism, they may also cut down production of natural duck-food plants which are much in demand by the feeding waterfowl. Manipulating water levels to produce food crops and meanwhile keep ducks healthy calls for expert timing plus an occasional bit of luck. The secret to the puzzle, says the refuge manager, "is flexibility and speed in water manipulation." And this is what the Fish and Wildlife Service was aiming at when it designed the water-control system for the Lower Klamath refuge. Water for this refuge comes from two sources. In early attempts to drain the lake, water from the Klamath River was cut off. The Fish and Wildlife Service once again directed the river waters into Klamath Lake. But still more water is brought in in a mile-long tunnel through Sheepy Ridge. Sheepy Ridge is a barren desert range of hills separating Tule Lake and Lower Klamath. When there is water to spare from Tule Lake eight large pumps lift it up to the tunnel. Once the water gets into the Lower Klamath refuge it is directed, as the refuge manager sees fit, into any of thirteen water-management areas, all separated from each other by dikes fitted with gates and valves.

All five refuges in the Klamath Basin are the responsibility of a single refuge manager. His biggest tasks are found at Tule Lake and Lower Klamath, because these are the most productive waters and the centers of the greatest concentrations of ducks and geese. Following a successful nesting season these two refuges may hold seven million ducks and geese at one time.

In recent times, with the drying up of potholes where the ducks nest to the north, their numbers have fallen in the Pacific Flyway, as elsewhere throughout the country. But the geese, on the other hand, nesting farther to the north in wilderness areas inhospitable to humans, have prospered. So geese on Tule and Klamath are increasing. The geese here may number three quarters of a million birds. In one recent autumn day refuge personnel censused 173,000 lesser snow geese on the two refuges, 227,-000 white-fronted geese, 11,500 Canada geese, 375,000 cackling geese and 1000 of the rare Ross's goose. In a recent ten-year period, the refuge records reveal an average of 78,000 waterfowl hatched here.

Most abundant of all the nesting ducks on this area is the redhead, which is becoming increasingly rare. Here in the broad marshes the gadwalls nest along with mallards, cinnamon teal, the little ruddy duck, and even a few pintails, scaup and canvasbacks. Drive along the State Line Road in midsummer and you can see them, whole families of half-grown ducklings shepherded by their mothers among the tules or out on the open water.

At other places on the five refuges are great colonies of black-crowned night herons, common egrets, and great blue herons. Several hundred pairs of double-crested cormorants build their nests in the trees along Thomas Creek in Upper Klamath refuge. Gulls, terns, herons and great numbers of white pelicans nest on islands in Clear Lake refuge. On Tule Lake three species of grebes, the eared, Western and pied-billed, all build their wet buoyant platform nests. For the five refuges the bird list records 250 species.

The pintail, prime tenant of Tule Lake, has long been a favorite with those who hunt ducks and those who watch them. The man in the duck blind knows the pintail as a bird that is graceful in flight and fast on the wing, and one that settles well to the decoys. And he also knows that the pintail rates high as table fare, an all-around prize that ranks with the mallard and the black duck.

The pintail feeds in the shallow waters where his long neck aids him in his efforts to pull roots and bulbs from the bottom of the marsh and search out small crustaceans. He tips down as though pivoted in the middle, his long graceful tail pointing to the sky and his webbed feet paddling rapidly to help him stand on his head. When he swims he holds his head high.

The male is the dandy with his white shirt, gray back and brown head. There is no mistaking him, but the female can, at casual glance, be easily mistaken for the hen gadwall or the female mallard.

Of all the ducks on the wintering marshes the pintails are among the first to leave in spring and start the long journey back to their breeding grounds in the north. Many of them nest in the wetlands of Alaska and over the western half of Canada from the Arctic Circle southward. The female pintail always builds her nest on dry ground, sometimes close, sometimes not so close, to water. And having chosen the spot, she lines the nest with down and deposits a clutch of eggs, usually fewer than ten. Finally, with all her eggs in place, she begins to incubate them, a chore she does not trust to her well-dressed mate. The ducklings hatch within twenty-two or twenty-three days. Once they are dry and able to waddle along behind her, she leads them toward the nearest water. There she soon teaches them which foods are meant for baby pintails. The male, somewhere nearby, does not seem greatly concerned by what should, by human standards, be his responsibility. The female does most of the family chores. She will even fight for her young or risk her life for their safety.

Once the young have acquired their full plumage, and the old birds have gone through the molt of late summer, they vacate their breeding grounds and head south. Eventually they come by the hundreds of thousands into the waiting barley fields and bulrushes of the Klamath Basin refuge complex.

If the refuges can withstand the incessant efforts of the irrigators to whittle away at the boundaries, waterfowl will continue to come to this historic valley to feed and rest in one of the most impressive natural dramas anywhere in the world.

Safety for the Desert Sheep

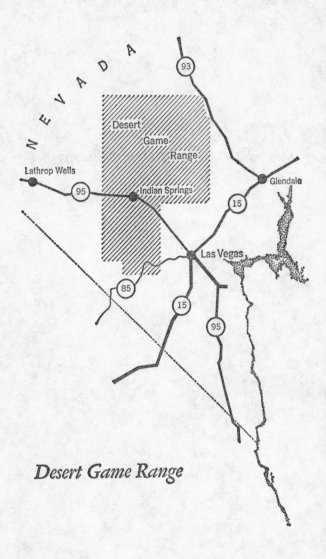

Desert Game Range

16

The bighorn sheep is wild of spirit. From the first hour of his life, when the mile-high winds dry his hair, he is at home on the rocky ledges far up in the broken slopes. Behind him is the sheer granite wall, beneath him a narrow shelf, and below the world is spread out in sweeping grandeur. One would think an animal relegated by nature to such inhospitable terrain would be off the path of the creeping human tide. But the story of the magnificent bighorn lacks this simple plot and happy ending.

As men advanced across the continent and invaded the wilderness regions, the bighorn sheep retreated. But nowhere did they find refuge from this resourceful two-legged predator. Especially hard-pressed were those separate races of bighorn sheep that, over the centuries, had learned to live in the high desert country.

The desert bighorn is a creature capable of firing the imagination of outdoorsmen everywhere. An adult bighorn ram has massive horns carrying almost a full curl. These horns alone may weigh thirty pounds and make up a fifth of the ram's weight, which on the Desert Game Range averages 160 pounds. Whether or not the desert bighorn really needs them to survive is speculative, but he has them, and from time to time he makes severe use of them, mostly during the mating season, which begins in June and lasts for five months.

For decades duels between competing bighorn rams have been billed as among the most fierce in the outdoors. But careful observers now believe the bouts may have been oversold. Ralph E. and Florence B. Welles, a husband-and-wife team of National Park Service naturalists, studied the bighorns of Death Valley over several years. "The concept of deadly enmity between rams with a battle to the death upon meeting," they reported, "could scarcely be further from the truth." The rams may let the whole thing go with a scuffle during which they arrange themselves head to rump and push each other around.

An encounter can, however, be dramatic and spectacular. On some occasions one of the contestants may abruptly turn and walk away. At this point the inexperienced bystander might consider the fight finished. But watch that ram left standing there alone. He knows better. The countdown is on.

The male who walked away may even lower his head as if to eat. Then he rears suddenly on his hind feet and comes barreling toward his opponent like a collision-bound steam locomotive. His opponent's head is down and ready. The rams collide with amazing accuracy and the clash of their horns may be heard a mile away.

Strangely enough the impact seems to cause neither any distress. The bout may end after a single blow or it may last an hour or two. The Welleses tell in *The Bighorn of Death Valley* of two rams that fought all of one day, during which they crashed forty-eight times. And still as far as observers could tell they showed no sign of shock or even a headache.

Where are the ewes, meanwhile? There may not even be one there to observe the duel. And if there is, a younger ram, or one whose mind is not on fighting, may capture the prize.

The ewes and their young ordinarily stay together in bands of a dozen or two. Their leader is an old female. Before the birth of her lamb the ewe wanders away from her band to the lambing ground, often at the base of a cliff or on a ledge. A single lamb is the rule and investigators have learned that the rate of increase on the Desert Game Range is sixty to seventy lambs per year for each one hundred ewes. April is the big month for lambing.

For several days the ewe keeps her new lamb near the spot where he was born and stands guard between him and the coyote, bobcat, golden eagle and mountain lion. Shortly, the lamb is scrambling over the rocks and along narrow trails with his mother as she rejoins the band. The lamb is weaned and living off the land by the age of six months. And the ram, through much of the year, is off somewhere by himself or with a little group of his kind, unbothered by any sense of family responsibility.

What is the origin of this wild sheep? Where did his ancestors roam? Scientists searching for clues to these puzzles have studied fossil remains and changing climates. "The bighorn sheep," as wildlife biologist Oscar Deming, told a gathering of the Desert Bighorn Council, "is a Johnny-come-lately on the North American continent. It is thought," he explained, "that he joined the rank and file of other assorted emigrants from Asia . . . as they crossed from Siberia to Alaska on the Bering land bridge during the middle of the Pleistocene Era, about 300,000 years ago." With them came others, including the bison, bear and elk.

"Somewhere toward the end of the line," says Deming, "came man, trailing along behind the herds, as befitting the herd hunter he was at that stage of his development.

"Arriving in his new home in the Southwest and Mexico, Ovis [the sheep] mingled with the native mammoths, mastodons, camels, antelope and species of horses, of which the largest one was found (naturally) in Texas.

"The bighorn found territory in the Southwest where he could exist in the rugged mountains of that land. And while other animals that came over with him, and some native species as well, perished and passed from the picture, the desert bighorn still lives there."

After the ancestors of the bighorns found their way

onto this continent and moved farther and farther south, they began to develop slight differences, depending on where they lived. In fact, they developed into two distinct species. One of these now occupies a limited range in the unglaciated parts of central Alaska. It became, not a "bighorn," but a "thinhorn," the Dall sheep, of which there are three races. The bighorns, ranging from the Canadian Rockies into northern Mexico, are divided into six races, which most people cannot tell apart and some of which can only be separated by learned scientists measuring skulls with calipers.

Largest of them all is the Rocky Mountain bighorn. Next comes the California bighorn of the Sierra Nevada and the Cascades. Then there are four desert races, including the Mexican bighorn, two races found in Lower California, and Nelson's bighorn. But in a family reunion of bighorn sheep, even the sheep might have trouble telling their cousins apart.

Deming spoke of the changing climate and the long-range troubles that may lie ahead for the desert bighorn. As the Wisconsin glacier, the last of the four great ice sheets, receded, it left behind a land of plenty, compared with that desert country today. There was more rainfall, there were tall grass prairies, and wild creatures, including the bighorn sheep, flourished.

There followed a period of geologic history when temperatures climbed and rainfall decreased. When this began, about eleven thousand years ago, it brought serious trouble for a long list of animals which could not adapt to the changing standards of living. From this continent some eighty-five species are known to have perished. The mastodons disappeared during the next five thousand years, as did the mammoths, camels and native horses. But not the bighorn sheep.

No new animals have come along since the Pleistocene. Those native animals here are ones that lived through those drastic climatic changes. "The bighorn sheep," says Deming, "in the Southwest and Mexico, watched the desert slowly creep up the mountain slopes and even over the top of much of its historical range, until it became a bighorn sheep living in the desert."

So, it may be true that the desert bighorn was already on the skids when the country was settled. His centuries may have been numbered.

But man numbered his hours.

The Indians hunted them by many methods. Sometimes they drove them into traps. Sometimes hunters hid in the hills, one on each peak, while tribesmen ran around the slopes below knowing that the bighorns would head for the high country.

The white man brought his own domestic sheep and with them scabies, a disease believed to have killed off great numbers of bighorns. But the white man brought guns as well, and there was uncontrolled hunting. When the gun would not produce lamb chops for the skillet, the desert miner or prospector propped up a door to trap sheep in the entrance of old mines where they came to find water.

There were Texas longhorns at the water holes, horses and burros in the hills, and ranches in the valleys across which the sheep had once migrated from one mountain range to another following seasonal sources of food and water. The bighorn never learned to prosper on the edge of man's holdings. Bands of sheep disappeared from one range after another. Eventually only those desert bighorns living in the most remote mountains remained. By 1930 there were no more than three hundred desert bighorns left in southern Nevada. And still there were poachers at the water holes.

North of Las Vegas lay great expanses of public domain. Hanging on in these arid hills were some of the few remaining desert bighorn sheep. In 1936, by presidential executive order, more than two million acres of that dry and starkly beautiful desert country was set aside to save the wild sheep. It was called the Desert Game Range. This refuge is an area bigger than Rhode Island: it stretches out eighty miles from north to south, and fifty miles from east to west. Today it provides living space for the largest remaining band of desert bighorns.

Then three years later, early in 1939, two additional executive orders established the Kofa Game Range and the Cabeza Prieta Game Range in the sun-baked desert of southern Arizona. Both of these were also for remnant bands of desert bighorns.

Within the two-million-acre Desert Game Range are six mountain ranges. They extend generally from north to south, and between the desert floor at the base of the mountains and the peaks are several life zones. Annual precipitation varies from two inches on the lowest altitudes to ten inches on the high slopes, and accounts for a wide variety of vegetation which, in turn, accounts for a wide variety of birds and mammals.

Highest point in the refuge is Charleston Peak, 11,910 feet above sea level, in the Spring Range west of Las Vegas. The best sheep country, however, is the Sheep Range extending along much of the eastern edge of the refuge due north of Las Vegas. It is one of the most barren of all the national wildlife refuges, so dry in many places that creosote plants are forty feet apart.

Biologists began studying the vegetation and the water supplies. It was their belief that the three hundred bighorns living there could be increased to six times as many and perhaps even more. Once they were protected from poachers, water was the biggest problem. The desert bighorns can survive on supplies of water so scant that one wonders how they can live. Even in the hottest part of summer they may visit a water hole only once every three or four days. Sometimes they chew the moist pulp of cactus, which Nature thought she protected with a coat of needle-sharp spines.

Refuge biologists concluded that a source of water every three to five miles would meet the needs of the sheep. In this country a spring that flows a gallon an hour is a treasure, and even the most insignificant seep becomes vitally important. To blast near one in an effort to increase the flow would risk sealing or draining it completely. The refuge staff has constructed about seventy watering devices on the refuge. Most of these are catchment basins to store water from seeps, in a concrete tank sunk into the hillside. Unauthorized livestock is sometimes fenced away from the water. The water may then be piped to a tank which can only be reached by way of a narrow ledge, no challenge to the sheep, impossible for the livestock. There is no need to worry about sheep finding the sources of water. On the Kofa Game Range they penetrate two hundred feet into the shaft of an abandoned mine to drink water collected from a seep.

In addition to their water problems, the bighorns, in some places, face a perpetual food shortage. Wild burros, deer, rodents and other animals pick at the same scant supplies. The desert bighorn subsists on scattered offerings of Apache plume, mountain mahogany, buckbush, grasses, and even the flowers and fruits of the barrel cactus and prickly pear.

The ever-growing population of humans in the desert may someday chase all the bighorns off the mountains. "Everybody thinks the refuge land out there isn't being used for anything," said refuge manager Newell B. Morgan, "and that he has a right to it." At least one cement company sought a permit for an open-pit mine that would allow prevailing winds to carry clouds of dust over some of the most productive lambing grounds on Sheep Mountain. Another organization, having decided to build itself a group camp in the heart of the range, had several miles of a three-lane highway built into the refuge before federal workers could stop them.

You hear the wildlife biologists say the refuge had three hundred sheep in 1936, and that this increased to seventeen hundred on the Desert Game Range by 1954. Or they may say there are eighteen hundred there today. How do they know? Their most trusted census method is the water-hole count which Oscar Deming worked out at the

Desert Game Range in 1947. For three blistering days in late June of 1956, every known water hole on the Desert Game Range was watched from dawn to dusk by cooperators from the refuge staff, National Park Service, Nevada Fish and Game Commission, Bureau of Land Management, Atomic Energy Commission (which studies the effects of fallout on wild animals) and the U. S. Air Force, which operates a practice bombing range on part of the refuge. Each evening the tracks around the water holes were smoothed over to detect any night drinkers.

From their observations and calculations the biologists concluded there were at least fifteen hundred sheep on the refuge but not more than seventeen hundred. Such census information is vitally important in managing the animals.

With sheep populations increasing, the inevitable question arose. Would hunting be permitted? If permitted to increase, the desert bighorn could cause the deterioration of its range, and reduce the bighorn carrying capacity of its desert home. The real challenge, of course, is for game managers to determine how many sheep the range can support. Then they must understand how rapidly the sheep reproduce and how many are lost to natural causes. Hunting is a logical method of taking any sheep that can still be spared. Dealing with a population as limited as that of the desert bighorn, however, calls for closely controlled hunting seasons.

The Nevada Fish and Game Commission works with the staff of the Desert Game Range to determine how many sheep should be taken by hunters and how the hunts should be managed. The first sheep hunt on parts of the Desert Game Range was in the spring of 1952 when forty-eight hunters took fifteen rams. Since then as many as eighty hunting permits have been issued for the annual hunts, and hunter success for the first nine hunts averaged 38.1.

Sheep hunting is for the rugged adventurer. Often the animals are at nine thousand feet. In these hunts only the rams with a three-quarter curl or better are legal. They have averaged 153 points measured by Boone and Crockett Club standards. Once the hunter is back with his animal, a team of technicians move in and the stomach is sacrificed for food-analysis studies, while such assorted bits of sheep anatomy as bladder, testicles and hock joints may be taken for still additional scientific study. There is a seemingly endless corps of researchers determined to uncover additional bits of information about the desert bighorn.

The bird list for this refuge is higher than visitors might expect; 227 species have been recorded. At the Corn Creek field station, twenty-six miles from Las Vegas, water from an artesian well has created an oasis in the desert. Waterfowl have been recorded here and nearly any time you can see Gambel's quail and road runners among the nearby Joshua trees. In some of the higher ranges of the refuge are mule deer and elk. There are coyotes, bobcats, foxes and sometimes a mountain lion.

The refuge has never been highly developed for recreational use. It is enough for this area to be the last stronghold of one of America's most rugged wild individuals, the desert bighorn sheep. The refuge that accomplishes this needs no recreational excuse for existence.

A single range of mountains could not have saved the bighorn. Depending on supplies of food and water, they move from one range to the other. In his corner of southeastern Nevada the bighorn has a lot of space, but he needs it.

Ralph and Florence Welles stated it perfectly before a gathering of the Desert Bighorn Council. "The wild sheep," they said, "the shy, elusive, magnificent bighorn we think about, needs room and freedom to be wild in—freedom from interference of all kinds—for any interference will change him a little from what he has been for the last eleven or twelve thousand years."

In an exhibition pen on the Desert Game Range I saw three desert bighorn sheep penned to help scientists better understand the wild sheep. A man could approach to within a few feet of them. These were not wild sheep; they were not wild anything. They were domesticated bighorns and not the same as the animal the Desert Game Range was created to preserve.

If we were content to keep them domesticated behind a wire fence, we would not need to offer them space. But unless we can save the wild spirit of the desert bighorn, we have saved only his shadow.

Tomorrow's Refuges

17

What of the future? The job is not yet done. Perhaps it is half done. If we are to witness the prosperity of waterfowl, or even see these birds hold their own, still new areas of wetlands must be added to the refuge holdings. As species become endangered, there will be need to provide what help we can toward lengthening their stay here.

Almost certainly, the nation's wildlife faces more hazards in the future than it has ever faced in the past. The human is just now, late in the twentieth century, on the threshold of a great breakthrough that will shortly double and triple his numbers on earth. At no time in history will the earth have been so densely covered with the supreme primate. Man, having gradually molded and modeled the world to his liking, now proceeds to smother it with his descendants. This specter casts a dark shadow. And standing in the shadow, with man, are all the lesser creatures.

With space at a growing premium, who will defend the wood duck or the bald eagle?

The wildlife refuges, maintained by states and private organizations as well as the federal government, provide safety for creatures that lived here before we came. They stand as a reservoir of laboratory space where future biologists may study the mysteries of protoplasm and the complexities of wild communities. On the major wildlife refuges there are opportunities for research that can bring

hope for the future of hard-pressed fish and game resources. Here are wildlife lands where government agencies could pool their resources for research into common
problems. "Too often," says refuge biologist Oscar Deming, "the federal refuges and state departments have gone
their separate ways, instead of joining forces on ecological
investigations, and both have fallen short of the maximum
potential because of duplication of work and effort."

The crisis in the wetlands may become increasingly severe. Private ownership of wetlands is becoming more
costly and difficult. Of the original 130 million acres of
open marshes in this country, some thirty million remain.
Waterfowl experts feel that twelve and a half million acres
must be preserved to do an adequate job for waterfowl.
Long-range plans are for the federal government to hold
eight million acres, and the states the other four and a half
million. This goal was set in the 1930s following a census
of the nation's wetlands. Thirty years after Ding Darling's
entrance into the scene in 1934, half of the job still lies
ahead of the refuge workers.

More recently another need has been emphasized if a
host of seldom seen and little known creatures are to be
rescued. The black-footed ferret faces extinction as the
prairie dogs on which he feeds are eliminated. Ross's
goose is in high danger. So is Bachman's warbler. Attwa-
ter's prairie chicken is now restricted to three Texas counties, and the lesser prairie chicken is in danger in New
Mexico, Oklahoma, Colorado and Texas. The ivory-billed
woodpecker may still exist in spite of widespread belief that
it is already extinct. In the Sierras the black toad is now
hanging on to a range that covers a single sixteen-acre
tract. On the verge of going out of existence are listed
112 cold-blooded species, twenty-four birds and fifteen
mammals. Most of them are not huntable, and consequently state conservation departments are unlikely to
spend hunting- and fishing-license money on their preservation.

Yet, there is widespread belief that any species which

can be saved from extinction should be preserved. "Think what man would have lost," said one biologist, "if the Rhesus monkey had been allowed to become extinct."

Some leading wildlife workers visualize a system of wildlife monuments, similar in concept to the historic and scenic national monuments administered by the National Park Service. Refuge workers have a list of 155 such monument areas, most of them small and planned for saving a single species. Congress or private agencies may someday set aside funds which would add these wildlife monuments to the already varied system of national wildlife refuges.

Meanwhile the bulk of the effort in behalf of wildlife on refuges will rightly continue to go to better-known animals, especially waterfowl. This, of course, is proper and logical because funds to buy and manage the waterfowl refuges come largely from the sale of duck stamps. For this reason some people who visit refuges equipped to hunt birds with camera and binoculars, stop at their post office once a year and buy their duck stamp. Even though they will never shoot a duck, they have then played a part in acquiring new wetlands and making them attractive to wildlife.

In the wildlife refuges we have cause for great national pride. Here we would not let the key deer or trumpeter swan disappear, or final disaster wipe out the desert bighorn. We have provided for the majestic elk, whooping crane, buffalo, and ducks and geese in wide variety.

And we have proved that, in a land of crop surpluses, great mines, fabulous factories, magnificent transportation systems, and impressive centers of culture and government, there is still room for wildlife.

Other Refuges Briefly Described

Each national wildlife refuge has its own story, distinctive features and interesting history. Those discussed in previous chapters were chosen for variety of wildlife, geographic locations and for the conservation stories found in their history. There are many more refuges that deserve such treatment. In the following pages are brief accounts of other wildlife refuges you may encounter in your travels. Most of those listed here have resident refuge managers.

Included in these thumbnail accounts are details on size of the refuge, numbers of birds found in the area, the species for which it was established, and some of the attractions visitors might find. Many of the refuges have fishing available in keeping with state regulations. On some hunting is permitted during special seasons. Camping is permitted in some refuge areas, but the facilities are never fancy, and most campers prefer to set up camp in nearby national forest, national park or state areas.

Nature study and bird watching are encouraged on nearly all refuges where human presence does not interfere with the welfare of wildlife. In these areas are some of the best remaining concentrations of wildlife anywhere.

ALABAMA

WHEELER, Box 1643, Decatur, Ala. 35601
This refuge of 34,000 acres, established in 1938 on one of
the TVA reservoirs, is primarily for geese and ducks.
Within twenty years geese on this refuge increased from a
few thousand to peaks of 85,000. There is fishing here for
crappie, bluegill, and bass. There are special hunts for
small game. The refuge bird list contains 250 species.

ALASKA

ALEUTIAN ISLANDS, Cold Bay, Alaska 99571

CLARENCE RHODE, Bethel, Box 346, Alaska 99559
This important waterfowl nesting refuge covers 2,870,000
acres of tundra on the coast of the Bering Sea. The area
became a refuge in 1960. Most of the black brant nest
here, as do emperor geese, whistling swans, shore birds
and little brown cranes. The refuge can be reached only
by chartered aircraft, upon approval of the refuge manager. There are no public accommodations.

KENAI NATIONAL MOOSE RANGE, Box 500, Kenai, Alaska
99611
This wildlife refuge of more than 1,730,000 acres was
established in 1941 for the management of the great Kenai
moose, brown bears, white sheep, mountain goats, and
trumpeter swans. The area comprises the western slopes of
the Kenai mountain range and the glacier-scarred lowlands bordering Cook Inlet. The trumpeter swans nest in
the lowlands. Campers, boaters and fishermen may use
the area without permit. In recent years extensive oil exploration has been permitted on part of this area.

KODIAK, Box 825, Kodiak, Alaska 99615
Covering two thirds of Kodiak Island, this wildlife refuge
of 1,815,000 acres was established in 1941 primarily for
the protection of the Kodiak bears, mule deer and water-

fowl. This is a famous area for the hunting of Alaskan brown bear. Wildlife biologists estimate that the Kodiak bear population on the refuge numbers about 1500. Also on this refuge are found several large rookeries of sea lions, which sometimes jump from twenty-foot cliffs into the sea when approached by humans. Sea otters also are found along the northern coast of this refuge. Visitors may enter the refuge without special permit. There are, however, no roads and most travel is by small plane.

ARTIC NATIONAL WILDLIFE RANGE, 1412 Airport Way, Fairbanks, Alaska 99701
In the northeastern corner of Alaska, bordered by the Arctic Ocean and the Yukon Territory, lies the biggest of all our national wildlife refuges. This is a land set aside for the wandering caribou, wolves, grizzly bears, giant moose, Dall sheep, and others. This refuge of 8,900,000 acres is without roads, and it has few human visitors. Oil, however, is the black shadow hanging over the Arctic National Wildlife Range. Conservationists believe this magnificent remnant of Arctic America should be declared an official wilderness area in an effort to bring lasting protection to its wildlife and wild lands.

ARIZONA

CABEZA PRIETA GAME RANGE, Box AP, Blythe, Calif. 92225
This desert refuge covering 860,000 acres was established in 1939 to bring protection to the endangered desert bighorn sheep. Also found here are the equally endangered Sonoran antelope, as well as Gambel's quail, the white-winged dove, mule deer and Javelina. The refuge's southern boundary is also the international boundary. Public use is discouraged, as the roads are mere trails, impassable except to four-wheel-drive vehicles. Visitors must have special permits from refuge headquarters. This is desert with scant rainfall and high summer temperatures.

HAVASU LAKE, Box A, Needles, Calif. 92363
Half in California and half in Arizona, this refuge of 45,700 acres was established in 1941 for the benefit of wild-

life, on the reservoir upstream from Parker Dam across
the Colorado River. The refuge extends fifty-five miles
north from the dam. Management includes brush control
and development of grazing areas for geese. Pintails and
green-winged teal begin to arrive by August. October
brings the Canada geese, snow geese, mallards, gadwalls,
pintails and American widgeons. This refuge is also home
to a wide variety of other wildlife, including hundreds of
thousands of tree swallows as well as nesting herons and
cormorants. Beaver are common. There are even a
few wild burros in the rugged mountains which in places
overlook the lake. Fishing is popular here for warm-water
species. Visitors boat, swim, water ski and camp. The bird
list includes 283 species. This is a big area and first-time
visitors may want to stop for information at any of the
eight concession areas.

IMPERIAL, Box AP, Blythe, Calif. 92225
This waterfowl marsh area of 46,791 acres was established in 1941. The refuge lies on both sides of the Colorado River where that stream forms the boundary between California and Arizona above Imperial Dam. The
refuge is about thirty-six miles long, and is superimposed
on an irrigation project. Campers may stay three days in
the concession areas. Fishing and boating are permitted,
except in posted wildlife areas. The bird list includes 250
species.

KOFA GAME RANGE, Box AP, Blythe, Calif. 92225
This range of 660,000 acres was also established in 1939,
as one of three areas for the desert bighorn. The band of
bighorns on the refuge numbers between 250 and 300
head. This is an area with spectacular rugged mountains,
and one of its canyons contains the only palm trees growing naturally in Arizona. Most roads are one-way trails,
difficult for any but four-wheel-drive vehicles. Visitors
should inquire at refuge headquarters.

ARKANSAS

BIG LAKE, Box 67, Manila, Ark. 72442
This refuge of 11,000 acres was secured in 1915 for the

protection of ducks and geese. The refuge headquarters is two and a half miles north of Manila on Highway 18. There is fishing for black bass, striped bass, crappie and bluegill. Squirrel hunting is permitted on one third of the refuge in accordance with state regulations. The refuge bird list contains more than 200 species. Wildlife-management practices here consist largely of the production of waterfowl foods and controlling water levels to prevent the spread of willows. There is swimming, fishing, boating and picnicking.

HOLLA BEND, Box 746, Russellville, Ark. 72801
This refuge, established in 1957, covers over 6367 acres and is largely used by ducks, geese, herons and bobwhites. There is fishing here for crappie and channel catfish. There are no camping facilities. More than 140 birds have been recorded here. Wildlife-management practices aim at improving habitat for migratory waterfowl. Old farmlands have been permitted to revert to woodlands and some have been farmed to provide waterfowl food. Pools have been constructed. Use of the area by wintering Canada geese is increasing.

WAPANOCCA, Box 257, Turrell, Ark. 72384
Established in 1961 for waterfowl, this refuge covers about 5484 acres. Visitors may fish. Hunting is not permitted. There are facilities for picnicking, and bird watchers are always welcome.

WHITE RIVER, Box 308, 704 S. Jefferson St., DeWitt, Ark. 72042
This refuge of 112,399 acres was acquired in 1935 primarily for ducks, geese, woodcocks, herons and wild turkeys. The refuge extends sixty miles along the White River and varies from three to eight miles in width. It is a concentration point for waterfowl passing down the Mississippi Flyway. In periods of high water 90 percent of this area is flooded. There are 90,000 acres of typical river-bottom hardwoods, including oak, gum, cypress and syca-more, excellent habitat, when flooded for migrating and wintering waterfowl. Fishermen catch catfish, crappie and black bass. Archers have a deer season here. There are facilities for campers and picnickers. Bird watchers have

recorded 214 species on the refuge. Farm practices produce feed crops for wintering flocks of more than 2000 Canada geese and thousands of ducks.

CALIFORNIA

KERN, Box 219, Delano, Calif. 93215
Purchased in 1960 for Canada geese and ducks, this refuge covers 10,600 acres. Nineteen miles west of Delano the road ends at the refuge entrance. There is no fishing, but public hunts are conducted for waterfowl. Years ago this area was part of a vast marsh and tule swamp, attracting millions of waterfowl, marsh birds and shore birds. Agricultural practices converted it to a desert. Refuge management is aimed at returning it to its former wetland character. Levees, canals and water-control structures have been planned and built. Waterfowl are now returning, although the water supply is limited. Pixley National Wildlife Refuge is also administered from Kern.

SACRAMENTO, Rte. 1, Box 311, Willows, Calif. 95988
This refuge, located seven miles south of Willows, covers 10,800 acres. It was purchased in 1937 for snow geese, cackling geese, whistling swans and ducks. This is an exceptionally important waterfowl refuge in the Pacific Flyway, and in winter it attracts a large part of the entire Pacific Flyway waterfowl population. Wild millet and rice are grown for waterfowl foods. Water levels are manipulated to promote the growth of emergent vegetation. There is fishing on the refuge for catfish, bass and sunfish. Pheasants are hunted. There are picnicking facilities. Bird watchers have counted 185 species here. Also administered by Sacramento personnel are three small areas: Colusa, 4040 acres; Delevan, 5300 acres; and Sutter, 2600 acres.

SALTON SEA, Box 247, Calipatria, Calif. 92233
Acquired by the government in 1930, and covering 35,200 acres, this is a refuge for ducks, geese and shore birds. Gradually much of its land area has been inundated by the steadily rising Salton Sea. The management plan now calls for raising alkali bulrushes in marsh-type artificial impoundments, helping hold the birds away from nearby commer-

cial crops. This refuge offers no fishing, but provides some waterfowl hunting. It is a good place for bird watching.

TULE LAKE, Box 74, Rte. 1, Tulelake, Calif. 96134

COLORADO

MONTE VISTA, Box 511, Monte Vista, Colo. 81144
This high desert refuge, six miles south of Monte Vista on Gunbarrel Road, covers 13,500 acres. Its purchase for waterfowl and sand-hill cranes was begun in 1952. Elevation here is 7500 feet. About 80 percent of this refuge is wet meadow and grazing land. Hunting, bird watching and fishing are permitted. Mallards, which both nest and winter here, sometimes reach peak levels of 70,000.

DELAWARE

BOMBAY HOOK, R.D. 1, Box 147, Smyrna, Del. 19977
Ten thousand of the 15,100 acres in this refuge are salt marshes. Purchased in 1937, it protects especially greater snow geese, black ducks, blue-winged teal and shore birds. This is a highly popular area for retriever trials. Some deer hunting is permitted. The bird list includes 302 species.

FLORIDA

CHASSAHOWITZKA, Rte. 1, Box 153, Homosassa, Fla. 32646
Purchased in 1943 for waterfowl, sand-hill cranes, limpkins and white ibises, this refuge covers 29,600 acres. Also found here are quail, turkey, deer and bear. Visitors are always welcome. There are 2500 acres open to waterfowl hunting under state regulations. Speckled-trout fishing is especially good here between September and April, while bass and bluegill fishing is productive throughout the year. The bird list includes 182 species.

J. N. "DING" DARLING, P.O. Drawer B, Sanibel, Fla. 33957
Established in 1945, this 4306-acre refuge is used by rose-ate spoonbills, herons, waterfowl and shore birds. The area is seventeen miles southwest of Fort Myers on Sanibel Island. Salt-water fishermen come for reds, snook, tarpon and speckled trout. Swimming and sunbathing is excellent here, and Sanibel beach is world-famous for its great variety of shells. Bird watchers have recorded 208 species and a special "bird tower" has been erected for the use of visiting bird lovers.

KEY DEER, Box 385, Big Pine Key, Fla. 33050

LOXAHATCHEE, Rte. 1, Box 278, Delray Beach, Fla. 33444
This 145,600-acre refuge was established in 1951 for waterfowl, sand-hill cranes, limpkins, herons, egrets and the endangered everglade kites. It is also an important alligator area. Management is aimed at protecting this Everglades habitat and its wildlife from poachers and invasion by pest plants. It is heavily populated by a wide variety of wildlife. Fishing is permitted, and species taken include bass, bream and crappie. The bird list includes 191 species.

PELICAN ISLAND, Box 6504, Titusville, Fla. 32780

ST. MARKS, Box 68, St. Marks, Fla. 32355
This area of 64,000 acres, is used by geese, ducks, herons, limpkins, wild turkeys and deer. It is Florida's only major wintering area for Canada geese. Artificial impoundments are heavily used by waterfowl. The refuge lies about thirty miles south of Tallahassee. Its acquisition was begun in 1931. This is a highly popular and productive fishing area, although parts of the refuge are closed to fishing during certain parts of the year to protect waterfowl. The refuge bird list includes 288 species.

GEORGIA

OKEFENOKEE, Box 117, Waycross, Ga. 31501

PIEDMONT, Round Oak, Ga. 31080
Acquired in 1939, this refuge covers 34,607 acres used by

waterfowl, bobwhites, wild turkeys and beavers. Since the establishment of the first impoundments on the refuge, duck use has increased more than 50 percent. Wild turkeys have increased from the few stocked in the 1940s to more than 250. The deer herd increased, within a ten-year period, from 120 animals to more than 1000. Because of this a public hunt for deer was initiated in 1960. Fishing here produces bass and bluegills. Birds recorded here total 159 species.

SAVANNAH, Rte. 1, Hardeeville, S.C. 29927
The 5500 acres in this refuge, established in 1927, are nearly equally divided between Georgia and South Carolina. Waterfowl, herons, otters, deer and alligators make use of Savannah Refuge. There is fishing for bream, crappie, bass and catfish. This is an excellent area for bird watching and has a list of well over 200 species. The refuge is ten miles up the Savannah River from the city of Savannah, and about twenty miles from the seacoast.

HAWAII

HAWAIIAN ISLANDS, 835 Akmus St., Kailua, Oahu, Hawaii 96734
This refuge was set aside in 1909 by President Theodore Roosevelt to protect the islands and their wildlife against unauthorized use, and to prevent the possible extinction of the unusual birds that live there. This chain of small Pacific islands and reefs extends more than 1100 miles between Hawaii and Midway. All but one of the islands in this chain are uninhabited. Hundreds of thousands of albatrosses, frigate birds, shearwaters, boobies, terns and other birds live on these islands. The remnant population of the rare Laysan duck is found on the island of Laysan. These islands are visited at infrequent intervals only by authorized refuge personnel. The continued protection of this chain of islands is considered extremely important.

IDAHO

CAMAS, Hamer, Idaho 83425
This refuge, located five miles northwest of Hamer, was acquired in 1937 and covers 10,500 acres. It is used by whistling swans, ducks, Canada geese, sage grouse, pheasants, long-billed curlews and pronghorn antelope. Six large irrigation pumps on this refuge provide the water supply. Land has been leveled and irrigated. Cereal crops are grown for waterfowl. No fishing is permitted. There is hunting for ducks, geese and pheasants.

DEER FLAT, Box 1457, Rte. 1, Nampa, Idaho 83651
This refuge on a reclamation area covers 11,400 acres and was established in 1909 for the use of Canada geese, ducks, white pelicans, and gulls. Wildlife management practices on this refuge include the conversion of former sagebrush and grassland to cereal-crop production for waterfowl. The grain is left standing to provide food for waterfowl in fall. Irrigated grass and alfalfa fields provide green feed for ducks and geese. Canada geese nest on islands in the Snake River. During mid-November when migration is at its peak there are often 750,000 ducks, mostly mallards, using this refuge. There is fishing for perch, bullheads, crappie and largemouth bass, and hunting for ducks, pheasants, quail, partridge and deer. Picnickers are welcome. The bird list includes 162 species.

MINIDOKA, Rte. 4, Rupert, Idaho 83350
The 25,600-acre Minidoka National Wildlife Refuge was established in 1909 for Canada geese, ducks, whistling swans and sage grouse. It is an overlay on a Bureau of Reclamation reservoir on the Snake River. Management practices here are largely aimed at waterfowl production. Crops for waterfowl food and cover have been planted, grazing and erosion controlled, and waterfowl nesting islands constructed. There is fishing for rainbow trout and yellow perch. Hunting is not permitted. The bird list includes 185 species.

ILLINOIS

CHAUTAUQUA, R.R. 2, Havana, Ill. 62644
This waterfowl refuge of about 5000 acres was purchased in 1936. During fall migration the population of ducks here may number one and a half million, making it one of the biggest concentration centers for waterfowl in the nation. The refuge bird list contains 236 species. This refuge is a well-known fishing area for crappie, bass, catfish and bluegills, and more than thirty thousand fishermen come here each year. There are facilities for picnicking and free boat launching. This area, which farmers once attempted to drain for farmland, has again become wetlands.

CRAB ORCHARD, Box J, Carterville, Ill. 62918
This famous refuge of 43,000 acres was established in 1947 by an Act of Congress. The law provides for recreation and for wildlife management, particularly for ducks and geese. It has since become one of the most heavily visited wildlife refuges in the country. Its recreational areas include facilities for hunting, fishing, swimming, picnicking, boating and camping. National field trials for hunting dogs are frequently held here. Thousands of visitors come in autumn to see the migrating concentrations of ducks and geese. Located as it is near the confluence of the Ohio and Mississippi rivers, Crab Orchard attracts great numbers of waterfowl and a wide variety of other birds. Over 100 of the 234 species of birds recorded on the refuge are known to breed here.

MARK TWAIN, Box 225, Quincy, Ill. 62013
Established in 1947 for ducks, geese, herons and shore birds, Mark Twain National Wildlife Refuge includes 14,-600 acres in the heart of the Mississippi River Valley. Within this refuge is the home of Tom Sawyer and Huckleberry Finn. The refuge lies along 250 miles of the great river and serves as a major link in the chain of waterfowl refuges in this flyway, which extends from Canada and Alaska to the Gulf of Mexico. The refuge's greatest im-

portance is as a wintering ground for mallards. Bald eagles winter here. Fishing is good for largemouth bass, bluegill, crappie and catfish. During the season of heaviest waterfowl use, usually October to April, the refuge is closed to fishing. Public use of the area during the rest of the year is encouraged, and there are facilities for picnicking, boating, hiking, bird watching and photography.

IOWA

UNION SLOUGH, Box 248, Titonka, Iowa 50480
This waterfowl refuge covers 2077 acres and was established in 1938. It is an important waterfowl migration stopover in north-central Iowa. No waterfowl hunting is permitted. However, an occasional deer season is held to keep the whitetails in check. A thirty-acre recreation area is open for picnics, swimming and fishing.

KANSAS

KIRWIN, Box 125, Kirwin, Kan. 67644
In 1954 the government established this 10,775-acre refuge for white-fronted geese, ducks, sand-hill cranes and shore birds. Through this area each fall pass hundreds of thousands of waterfowl migrating down the Central Flyway. Many stop for the entire winter, when the bird population includes up to 75,000 mallards and 5000 Canada geese. Waterfowl may be seen here almost any time of year. Although there is no hunting on this refuge, fishing, boating and camping are permitted. Within the refuge is a 5000-acre lake, some 2600 acres of farmland and 3300 acres of rangeland. Cultivated food crops are grown for waterfowl. Some 250,000 people visit this refuge each year and more than 100,000 of them come to fish for largemouth bass, channel catfish, crappie, bluegill and walleyes. More than 179 species of birds have been recorded on Kirwin National Wildlife Refuge.

QUIVIRA, Box G, Stafford, Kan. 67578
This refuge of 21,800 acres was established in 1955 and is

maintained primarily for waterfowl. Lying in the Central Flyway, the refuge includes marshes, rangeland, farmlands and sand hills. The refuge bird list contains 245 species. There is no hunting, fishing or boating.

LOUISIANA

Delta, 1216 Amelia St., Gretna, La. 70053
Blue geese, snow geese, ducks, egrets, shore birds and alligators are the major species benefiting from this 48,800-acre refuge seventy miles south of New Orleans on the delta of the Mississippi River. It was acquired in 1935 for wintering waterfowl, which number 120,000 snow geese and 130,000 ducks in spite of more than 160 producing oil wells on the refuge. No public recreation facilities are found here. Visitors must first contact the refuge manager, since travel is by boat. The bird list includes 212 species.

Lacassine, Rte. 1, Box 186, Lake Arthur, La. 70549
This refuge, established in 1937, is one of the southernmost refuges in the chain of wildlife areas the federal government has established along the Mississippi Flyway. It covers 31,700 acres, used largely by blue geese, snow geese, mottled ducks, spoonbills, anhingas and ibises. The bird list includes 228 species. Management practices consist of controlling water levels, grazing and burning and farming. Grazing and burning keeps vegetation down and provides tender green browse for geese. These practices and the natural attractiveness of the area to waterfowl have resulted in one of the largest concentrations of ducks in the Mississippi Flyway. There is fishing for black bass, bream and white perch. There is no hunting or picnicking.

Sabine, MRH 107, Sulphur, La. 70663
Sabine was acquired in 1937 and includes 142,850 acres managed and protected for blue geese, snow geese, mottled ducks, roseate spoonbills, glossy ibises and alligators. This refuge has one of the largest remaining populations of alligators in the country. Control of alligator poaching is a major refuge problem. Great flocks of blue and snow geese congregate here in winter and reach peak

populations during December and January. The annual Christmas bird count on and around the Sabine refuge totals some 150 species, one of the longest lists in the country. The bird list includes 308 species. There is no hunting or picnicking. Fishing is permitted and the species taken include bass, bluegill, crappie and catfish.

MAINE

MOOSEHORN, Box X, Calais, Maine 04619
Established in 1937 for woodcock, black ducks and ring-necked ducks, Moosehorn covers 22,565 acres at the eastern tip of Maine. Much of the 22,000 acres in this refuge is in pine, spruce and hardwood forests, interspersed with lakes, streams and marshes. Adjacent to it are several miles of rugged, rocky seacoast. Fine roads and trails cross this refuge, helping to make it popular with visiting bird watchers and trout fishermen. The bird list includes 218 species. There is a recreation area where visitors sometimes dig their own clams for a picnic dinner. There are 150 picnicking and camping sites.

MARYLAND

BLACKWATER, Rte. 1, Box 121, Cambridge, Md. 21613
Established in 1933, this 11,200-acre refuge is on the east shore of Chesapeake Bay, ten miles southeast of Cambridge. It is maintained primarily for Canada geese, muskrats, snow geese and ducks. The bird list includes 231 species. From a population of 5000 Canada geese in 1942 the refuge wintering goose flock has increased to more than 80,000. Because this refuge is close to highly populated areas, it is visited each year by thousands of people interested in observing wildlife.

MASSACHUSETTS

MONOMOY, 191 Sudbury Rd., Concord, Mass. 01742
Monomoy, purchased in 1944, has 2700 acres largely for

the use of black ducks, eiders, scoters and shore birds. It is located on the elbow of Cape Cod approximately 100 miles southeast of Boston and 285 miles northeast of New York City. Most of the refuge can be reached only by water. It is considered by the Fish and Wildlife Service to be an important link in its chain of Atlantic Flyway refuges. Management includes rehabilitation of marsh areas, plantings of wildlife food crops, maintenance of potholes and dune-erosion control. Among the fish that can be taken off this famous fishing spot are striped bass from May through October, bluefish from August through September, flounder and fluke with seasons running from June through September, cod all year and haddock from May through November.

PARKER RIVER, Northern Boulevard, Newburyport, Mass. 01950
This refuge, purchased in 1942, contains 4650 acres for black ducks, greater scaup, Canada geese and shore birds. Headquarters is on Plum Island, two miles north of the refuge. Surf fishing, especially for striped bass, is popular here. The public recreation area provides an excellent sand beach. This is a popular area for bird watching, painting and photography. The refuge bird list contains 302 species.

MICHIGAN

SENEY, Seney, Mich. 49883
This refuge, sprawling over 95,500 acres of the Great Manistique Swamp, was purchased in 1935 primarily for Canada geese, ducks and sand-hill cranes. More than half of the area is wetland, with some 7000 acres impounded in twenty man-made pools by a network of dikes. It has become a nesting area for Canada geese. During the summer season visitors may take one of the conducted tours over the ten-mile-long nature trail through interesting parts of the refuge. Fishing is permitted. The refuge bird list contains 226 species.

SHIAWASSEE, 6975 Mower Road, Rt. 1, Saginaw, Mich. 48601
In 1953 the government began acquiring the Shiawassee

refuge of 8800 acres. The State of Michigan administers the adjacent state area known as the Shiawassee River State Game Area. The refuge is used as a feeding and resting area for thousands of geese and ducks.

MINNESOTA

AGASSIZ, Middle River, Minn. 56737

RICE LAKE, McGregor, Minn. 55760
Covering 20,296 acres, this refuge, established in 1935, is especially important to mallards, ringneck ducks and beaver. The refuge lies in a low boggy area. Indian tribes hunted here and gathered the wild rice for which the area is well-known. Summer fishing is good for northern pike. Rare birds seen in recent years include the Western bluebird, black-billed magpie, white pelican, green heron and Caspian tern. The refuge bird list includes 212 species. Muskrats, mink, beaver, otter and raccoons are trapped here under permit.

TAMARAC, Rochert, Minn. 56578
In 1938 the government purchased this 42,500-acre refuge for ducks and geese using the Mississippi Flyway. Also found on this refuge are deer, ruffed grouse, muskrats and beaver. More than two thirds of the refuge is timber, predominately aspen, birch and conifers. Public recreation is permitted on the refuge, providing it does not interfere with waterfowl management. Fishing is permitted on refuge lakes during much of the Minnesota season.

MISSISSIPPI

NOXUBEE, Rte. 1, Brooksville, Miss. 39739
Noxubee was acquired in 1940 and contains 45,700 acres primarily for the protection of waterfowl and wild turkeys. Management practices on this refuge are directed at feeding migrating waterfowl. Cereal food crops are grown for wildlife. Construction of levees has created new wintering grounds for thousands of ducks. A type of management known as "green tree reservoirs," pioneered at Noxubee

National Wildlife Refuge, has brought great increases of waterfowl to the flooded timberlands during fall and winter. This plan provides excellent duck wintering habitat, using dikes and water-control devices to flood timbered autumn lands. Fishing is permitted during the season for largemouth bass, bream, crappie and catfish. There are only limited facilities for picnicking. The bird list contains 205 species.

YAZOO, Rte. 1, Box 286, Hollandale, Miss. 38748
This refuge, covering 12,470 acres, was established in 1936. It was purchased for Canada geese, ducks and herons. The area is managed primarily for the establishment of wintering Canada-goose flocks, which requires the production of agricultural food crops, and the impoundment of water. There are public dove and squirrel hunts, usually in September and early October, by permit. Fishing is available here for sunfish, largemouth bass and channel catfish. Observers have recorded 132 species of birds on this refuge.

MISSOURI

MINGO, Rte. 1, Box 9A, Puxico, Mo. 63960
Mingo, established in 1944, covers 21,650 acres important to geese, ducks and herons. Refuge headquarters is one and a half miles northeast of Puxico on Highway 51. This refuge, on the east edge of the Ozarks, consists of lowland bordered by limestone bluffs and rolling hills. Migrating waterfowl, often 90 percent mallards, begin arriving the first week of November. Peak populations may include 140,000 ducks. Water levels are manipulated to encourage the natural growth of waterfowl food plants. About 3500 acres of corn, sorghum, soybeans, wheat and rice are grown for wildlife foods. Fishermen make good use of this refuge. Conducted tours are made each week in November so visitors may see and photograph the great concentrations of waterfowl.

SQUAW CREEK, Box 101, Mound City, Mo. 64470
This 6800-acre refuge, acquired in 1935, attracts thou-

sands of blue and snow geese, ducks and white pelicans. The area was once part of a large natural marsh in the Missouri River bottoms. Drainage of these lands for agriculture once practically ruined them for waterfowl use but they have been returned to part of their original wetland condition. About 100,000 mallards and 5000 Canada geese winter here. Hundreds of fishermen come to this refuge each year. The Squaw Creek bird list includes 265 species.

SWAN LAKE, Box 68, Sumner, Mo. 64681
Purchased primarily for the preservation of Canada geese, ducks and prairie chickens, this national wildlife refuge of 10,675 acres was established in 1937. It provides a resting and feeding area for one of the largest single concentrations of Canada geese in North America. At times there may be 130,000 of these birds on the Swan Lake refuge. There are also thousands of other waterfowl and shore birds. With the help of the Civilian Conservation Corps, beginning in 1937, levees and water-control structures were built, land was cleared and roads and buildings were constructed. Five thousand acres of marsh have been improved for waterfowl and 3000 acres are farmed for wildlife food crops. Part of the refuge is open to the public for fishing in summer. The catch consists mostly of channel catfish, bullhead, carp and drum. The bird list contains more than 216 species.

MONTANA

BENTON LAKE, Box 2646, Great Falls, Mont. 59401
Created in 1929 for waterfowl, this refuge covers 12,400 acres. Refuge headquarters is fourteen miles northeast of Great Falls. This is primarily a waterfowl refuge.

BOWDOIN, Box J, Malta, Mont. 59538
Refuge headquarters is seven and a half miles east of Malta and one-fourth mile south of Highway 2. This area was established in 1936. It includes 15,500 acres of importance primarily to Canada geese, ducks, white pelicans, herons, cormorants and sage grouse. Management prac-

tices have included diking of three large impoundments totaling 7620 acres. These provide excellent nesting, resting and feeding habitat for great numbers of migratory waterfowl. There is no fishing on this refuge, but a total of 4040 acres is open to waterfowl hunters. The bird list includes 168 species.

CHARLES M. RUSSELL NATIONAL WILDLIFE RANGE, Box 110, Lewistown, Mont. 59457
Established in 1936 as the Fort Peck Game Range, it provides for sharp-tailed grouse, sage grouse, pronghorn antelope, deer, bighorn sheep, elk and waterfowl. This important refuge includes 926,500 acres. Improvement of waterfowl habitat in recent years has resulted in a steady increase in the numbers of ducks and geese using the area. This refuge lies on either side of the Fort Peck Reservoir and extends for 220 miles along the Missouri River. It is a rugged area of extreme erosion and high grassy plateaus surrounded with conifers. Fishing is permitted for bluegill, channel catfish, sturgeon, paddlefish, northern pike, rainbow trout and walleyes. Hunters may take deer, elk and migratory waterfowl during the seasons. The U. S. Army Corps of Engineers maintains improved camping areas and boat-docking facilities around the Fort Peck Reservoir. The bird list includes 263 species.

MEDICINE LAKE, Medicine Lake, Mont. 59247
Established in 1935, this refuge of 31,500 acres provides habitat for geese, ducks, sand-hill cranes, sharp-tailed grouse and shore birds. This is in the Great Plains section of the country and development of nesting and rearing habitat has attracted thousands of ducks and helped establish a resident flock of Canada geese. There is fishing for a wide variety of species. There are 2700 acres open to waterfowl hunting, and 2200 acres open to deer hunting. The bird list includes 186 species.

NATIONAL BISON RANGE, Moiese, Mont. 59824
Here, in 1908, President Theodore Roosevelt set aside 18,-540 acres for the preservation of buffalo, elk, deer, bighorn sheep, waterfowl and shore birds. The major problem of the refuge manager here is to maintain good range for the big-game animals. This has been accomplished so well that

the area is an outstanding example of good range management. No fishing or hunting is permitted. The bird list includes 171 species. Visitors may go on a two-hour guided tour daily from June 20 through Labor Day. The tour includes the exhibition pastures for bison and other native big-game animals.

NINE-PIPE and PABLO, Moiese, Mont. 59824
These two small refuges lie fifteen miles apart between the Bitterroot and Mission mountain ranges in northwestern Montana. They became wildlife refuges in 1921. Fall waterfowl populations may build up to 200,000 birds. From May to October many species of water and marsh birds nest on the refuges. The bird list includes 161 species. Fishing is permitted on the areas except for portions closed during waterfowl nesting seasons.

RED ROCK LAKES, Star Rt. 1, Lima, Mont. 59739

NEBRASKA

CRESCENT LAKE, Ellsworth, Neb. 69340
This refuge was purchased in 1931 for geese, ducks, sandhill cranes, long-billed curlews and other water birds. It covers 46,000 acres in the sand hills of Nebraska. The area consists of small lakes and rolling hills in a land that is predominately grazing country. A great variety of waterfowl migrate through here and the refuge is also used by nesting ducks and prairie grouse.

FORT NIOBRARA, Valentine, Neb. 69201
Covering 19,122 acres, this area was set aside in 1912 largely for the protection of buffalo, Texas longhorn cattle, elk, prairie chickens and sharp-tailed grouse. It is made up of rolling grasslands along the scenic Niobrara River. Some buffalo and elk are kept in exhibition pastures. The government's second largest herd of Texas longhorn cattle is maintained on this refuge. The herds are rounded up each year in October for branding and vaccinating. This is a famous area for fossil beds, and some twenty extinct species of animals have been unearthed, collected and

classified for display in the refuge museum. There is a
public recreation area.

VALENTINE, Valentine, Neb. 69201
The 71,516 acres in this refuge were purchased in 1935
for ducks, geese, sharp-tailed grouse, pheasants, shore
birds and pronghorn antelope. Located in the sand hills of
Nebraska, it provides a resting and nesting area for Central
Flyway waterfowl. Fishing here is for bass, bluegills,
northern pike and walleyes. More than 224 species of birds
have been recorded. In October the waterfowl population
is likely to exceed 75,000 birds.

NEVADA

DESERT NATIONAL WILDLIFE RANGE, 1500 N. Decatur
Blvd., Las Vegas, Nev. 89108

RUBY LAKE, Ruby Valley, Nev. 89833
This refuge for Canada geese, ducks, sage grouse and
shore birds was established in 1938. It lies sixty miles south
and east of Elko, Nevada, at the foot of the Ruby Mountains. It covers 37,600 acres. This is one of the few
places where visitors see trumpeter swans. Public recreational use of the refuge is growing each year. There is
fishing for rainbow, brown and brook trout, and also for
largemouth bass. Trout fishing is best in spring and fall.
Units on the refuge have been developed for the use of
Canada geese and such ducks as canvasback and redheads
which feed on the natural foods and supplemental waterfowl crops, especially barley, planted on the uplands.

STILLWATER, Box 592, Fallon, Nev. 89406
Created in 1948, this refuge of 24,200 acres provides protection for whistling swans, geese, ducks, herons and shore
birds. Marshes and ponds are maintained for waterfowl,
marsh birds and shore birds in great numbers. There are
on the refuge limited facilities for hunting, fishing, camping, boating and picnicking. An additional 200,000 acres
are managed jointly with the Trukee-Carson Irrigation
District and the Nevada Game Commission as the Stillwater Wildlife Management Area.

NEW JERSEY

BRIGANTINE, Box 72, Oceanville, N.J. 08231

NEW MEXICO

BITTER LAKE, Box 7, Roswell, N.M. 88201
This refuge was purchased in 1937 primarily for waterfowl and sand-hill cranes. It covers 23,000 acres. The refuge is on the Pecos River fifteen miles northeast of Roswell. In the fall more than twenty species of waterfowl come to these lakes, ponds and marshes. Ordinarily there are 50,000 ducks and geese resting and feeding on the refuge. Most common among the waterfowl are the mallards, American widgeons, pintails and canvasbacks. Public hunting of waterfowl is ordinarily permitted on 450 acres south of the lake. No boats are permitted, but fishing is ordinarily allowed in summer months. The area has six impoundments where white bass, largemouth bass and channel catfish are taken. The refuge bird list contains over 200 species.

BOSQUE DEL APACHE, Box 278, San Antonio, N.M. 87832
This refuge, established in 1939, covers 57,200 acres. It was purchased primarily for ducks, geese, Gambel's quail and sand-hill cranes. It is the only refuge of its kind on the Rio Grande. It is above Elephant Butte Reservoir, in the central part of New Mexico, about seventy-five miles south of Albuquerque. Over 13,000 acres of this refuge are river bottomlands. Undesirable brush and trees have been removed from 5500 acres. Dikes, canals and water-control structures have been constructed on these management units. Some 44,000 upland acres of Bosque Del Apache are predominately desert country. The bird list here includes more than 260 species. On designated parts of the refuge, in favorable years, fishing and quail hunting are permitted in keeping with state regulations.

SAN ANDRES, Box 756, Las Cruces, N.M. 88001
Established in 1941, this refuge contains 57,215 acres. It

was set aside for desert bighorn sheep, mule deer, Gambel's quail and scaled quail. This is an area of typical desert vegetation. When the refuge was established, there were thirty-three bighorn sheep remaining here. Within a few years these had increased to 140 animals. Some have since moved out and repopulated adjacent areas. Found here also are mountain lions, bobcats and coyotes. Mule-deer hunts are held on the refuge. Except for deer-hunting seasons, the refuge, which lies within the White Sands Missile Range and is subject to security regulations, is closed to public use.

NEW YORK

MONTEZUMA, R.D. 1, Seneca Falls, N.Y. 13148
Montezuma, which was purchased in 1938 and contains 6400 acres, was established for the protection of ducks, geese, muskrats and deer. It lies at the north end of Cayuga Lake in the Finger Lakes region of New York State. The refuge headquarters is one hundred miles east of Buffalo and five miles northeast of Seneca Falls. Open marsh, swamp, woodland and cultivated fields provide habitat for waterfowl. Eight miles of earthen dikes have been constructed on this refuge. These trap the waters from several small streams to form about 3000 acres of marsh. Water levels here can be controlled to help produce natural supplies of waterfowl foods. The bird list includes more than 250 species. Mallards, wood ducks, black ducks, gadwalls, shovelers, redheads and ruddy ducks are commonly seen. Fishing is limited to small areas to prevent interference with waterfowl production.

MORTON, Target Rock Rd., Huntington, N.Y. 11743
Donated to the Bureau of Sport Fisheries and Wildlife in 1954 for black ducks, shore birds, gulls and terns, this refuge one hundred miles east of New York City covers only 187 acres. There is good fishing in the waters around the refuge, and boat harbors nearby can supply boats and equipment. Shellfishing is permitted in the shallow waters along the shores. There are no facilities for recreational use. In spite of its small size nearly 200 species of birds

have been recorded on this refuge. Common waterfowl include black ducks, mallards, scaups, old-squaws, buffle-heads and goldeneyes.

NORTH CAROLINA

MATTAMUSKEET, New Holland, N.C. 27885
This famous waterfowl wintering area was purchased in 1934. It covers 50,177 acres. Canada geese, whistling swans and ducks congregate here in great numbers. Nearby is the 15,500-acre Swan Quarter National Wildlife Refuge, which was secured two years later. The managed waterfowl hunts on Mattamuskeet are famous and draw hunters from many states. Sport fishing is also possible in this area. Mattamuskeet Lodge in the refuge is concessionaire-operated. The north border of the refuge is rimmed with cypress trees. The south shore, however, is low marsh country. Here one can see the largest gathering of Canada geese on the Atlantic seaboard, and perhaps the greatest number of whistling swans assembled anyplace. After it was acquired by the federal government, steps were taken to return this drained area to its original wetland nature. Since that time control of wetlands, water levels and vegetation have helped make it increasingly attractive for waterfowl. Bird watchers have found more than 230 species here.

NORTH DAKOTA

ARROWWOOD, R.R. 1, Edmunds, N.D. 58434
This is a 16,000-acre waterfowl refuge acquired in 1935. Whistling swans, geese, ducks and sharp-tailed grouse use it. This is one of the chain of refuges that extend along the Central Flyway. Swimming and picnicking are permitted. Fishing is primarily for northern pike, walleyes, yellow perch and bullheads. The bird list numbers over 200 species.

DES LACS, Box 578, Kenmare, N.D. 58746
Des Lacs, covering 18,881 acres, was acquired in 1935 for

ducks, geese, grebes and sharp-tailed grouse. There have been extensive plantings of marsh and aquatic vegetation to provide food and cover for waterfowl. Middle Des Lacs Lake stores runoff snow water. Water levels are artificially controlled to speed the growth of waterfowl food plants. This refuge, because of its inclusion in the Souris River group of refuges, is considered especially important to migrating waterfowl in the Central Flyway. There are picnicking and camping facilities two miles west of Kenmare. Deer hunting is permitted during the regular state seasons if the refuge herd warrants the reduction. Fishing is permitted in a portion of the upper lake, but the fishing is not particularly good, largely because of the shallow water and the resulting winter kill.

LAKE ILO, Dunn Center, N.D. 58626
This waterfowl refuge was secured in 1939. It covers 4040 acres. There is a public park on the shore of Lake Ilo where visitors may swim, boat or fish.

LONG LAKE, Moffit, N.D. 58560
Long Lake includes 22,300 acres. It was purchased in 1932 and is heavily used by ducks and geese. Here also are found gulls, pheasants, gray partridges and sharp-tailed grouse, as well as shore birds and sand-hill cranes. Located in south-central North Dakota, this refuge is composed largely of typical prairie grasslands, ravines and cultivated fields, as well as a shallow natural lake. The annual rainfall averages less than seventeen inches. A major problem here is the control of botulism. Common nesting ducks are mallards, gadwalls, pintails and blue-winged teal. During the migration period large numbers of Canada geese and white-fronted geese come through this area. The best times to see wildlife at Long Lake, especially waterfowl and shore birds, are April and May and again in September and October. Sport fishing is permitted in four areas of the refuge from mid-May to mid-September. Sand-hill cranes begin to arrive at Horseshoe Lake, near the refuge, in late September and soon build to several thousand on their way to New Mexico and Texas for the winter. As a supplement to natural waterfowl foods such as hard-stemmed

bulrush, prairie bulrush and sago pondweed, 900 acres of
the refuge are cultivated.

LOSTWOOD, R.R. 1, Lostwood, N.D. 58745
Covering about 26,750 acres, Lostwood National Wildlife
Refuge was established in 1935 primarily for the benefit
of waterfowl. Sharp-tailed grouse and sand-hill cranes, as
well as shore birds and muskrats, are also abundant. This
refuge is one of the typical prairie pothole areas of the
United States, a natural historic breeding ground for waterfowl. Its numerous small lakes and potholes make it
one of the best waterfowl production refuges in the Central Flyway. Because of its importance as a waterfowl and
shore-bird nesting area there are no public-use facilities.

J. CLARK SALYER, Upham, N.D. 58789
This famous and important waterfowl refuge covers 58,-
700 acres of river-bottom marsh with surrounding upland
area. It was acquired in 1935. Migrating waterfowl assemble here by the hundreds of thousands in the fall. It is also
an exceptionally productive waterfowl nesting area. Hunting, fishing and picnicking are permitted at certain periods
of the year and in keeping with state regulations. This is
another of those areas once drained and destroyed as
waterfowl habitat, and eventually returned to its wetland
nature. More than 250 species are found on its bird list,
and 123 species have been known to nest here. The bird
list includes 27 species of ducks, 27 warblers, 36 finches,
and 34 kinds of shore birds. Mallards and pintails are the
most important waterfowl in Lower Souris. In those years
when a surplus of whitetail deer exists on the refuge there
is a controlled hunt in keeping with state regulations.

SLADE, Dawson, N.D. 58428
This 3000-acre waterfowl refuge was given to the government in 1944. Here the rolling prairie, dotted with lakes
and potholes, is used by waterfowl seven months of the
year for resting, feeding and nesting. There are recreational facilities at the Lake Isabel area.

SULLYS HILL NATIONAL GAME PRESERVE, Fort Totten,
N.D. 58335
This is one of four fenced big-game preserves adminis-

tered by the Fish and Wildlife Service. Acquired in 1914 for buffalo, elk, deer and geese, this refuge contains 1675 acres. The area is given over largely to rolling country of timbered hills and grassy meadows.

TEWAUKON, R.R. 1, Cayuga, N.D. 58013
Covering 7447 acres, this waterfowl refuge was purchased in 1945. Refuge work here is aimed at turning this typical rolling prairie country of lakes, marshes and uplands into a better nesting, feeding and resting area for migratory waterfowl. Fishing is popular.

UPPER SOURIS, R.R. 1, Foxholm, N.D. 58738
One of the country's most important waterfowl production areas, this refuge, covering 32,085 acres, was secured in 1935 for ducks and geese, as well as sharp-tailed grouse, prairie chickens and sand-hill cranes. The largest body of water on it is Lake Darling, which extends from the dam at headquarters northward for twenty miles. It supplies water for the marshy impoundments downstream, especially the marshes of the Lower Souris refuge forty miles to the east. This lake was designed to hold a two-year water supply. The Souris chain of wildlife refuges is an outstanding example of refuge planning. Peak waterfowl populations occur in September and October when there are often more than 50,000 birds on this refuge. Stopping here are whistling swans and four species of geese, as well as great flocks of mallards. Parts of Lake Darling are open to public fishing, and fishermen come from considerable distances to try for the northern pike, which frequently weigh more than twenty pounds. More than 250 species of birds are found on the Souris Loop refuges.

OHIO

OTTAWA, R.R. 3, Box 269, Oak Harbor, Ohio 43449
The first lands were purchased in 1961 for this refuge. It includes some of the finest remaining waterfowl habitat in the marshes along the southern edge of Lake Erie. It will ultimately contain 5500 acres. Adjacent to it is the highly productive 2500-acre McGee Marsh Wildlife Area, ad-

ministered by the State of Ohio. The waterfowl most commonly seen here are mallards, black ducks, scaups, Canada geese and American widgeons.

OKLAHOMA

SALT PLAINS, Rt. 1, Box 49, Jet, Okla. 73749
Acquisition of this refuge began in 1930. It contains over 32,000 acres heavily used by geese, ducks and white pelicans. Salt deposits on the flats provided a natural source for both man and wildlife in the past. More than 200,000 visitors come to this refuge each year, to fish, swim or boat. There are limited picnicking and camping facilities. The commonly caught fish are channel catfish and black bass. Field-dog trials are frequently held here. During periods of migration there may be more than 150,000 ducks in this area and 40,000 may spend the winter. Mallards are the most abundant, followed by pintails and green-winged teal. This is also an important area for geese, both those passing through and those that come to spend the winter. The wintering geese have sometimes numbered 9000. More than three million Franklin's gulls are usually here during the fall migration. The refuge bird list numbers more than 250 species.

TISHOMINGO, Box 248, Tishomingo, Okla. 73460
This 16,400-acre wildlife area was established in 1946 primarily for the use of ducks, geese and shore birds. Located on an area of Lake Texoma, it is highly popular for fishing. Crappie and channel catfish are the most commonly taken species. More than 225 species of birds have been recorded on this refuge and on the nearby Hagerman National Wildlife Refuge in Texas.

OREGON

HART-SHELDON REFUGES, Box 111, Lakeview, Ore. 97630

MALHEUR, Box 113, Burns, Ore. 97720
Malheur, established in 1908, covers 180,850 acres. It is important to whistling swans, ducks, sand-hill cranes and

white pelicans, as well as shore birds and a small herd of pronghorn antelope. Marshes, meadows and shallow lakes surrounded by sagebrush and juniper uplands characterize this refuge. This is an outstanding waterfowl area with a high rate of production for several species. There is a museum where visitors may study mounted bird specimens and there is also a display pool with a photographer's blind at refuge headquarters. Fishing is permitted on Krumbo Lake, and in some seasons there is waterfowl hunting as well as archery hunting for deer. More than 230 species of birds occur, including whistling swans, snow geese, mallards, pintails and gadwalls in great numbers. Trumpeter swans nest on this refuge. Besides fishing for rainbow trout there is hunting for deer and waterfowl. Management practices are designed to benefit waterfowl by production of cereal crops, manipulation of water levels and elimination of sagebrush and willow growth.

THREE ARCH ROCKS, Willapa Wildlife Refuge, Ilwaco, Wash. 98624

PENNSYLVANIA

ERIE, R.D. 2, Box 197, Guys Mills, Pa. 16327
Land acquisition began here in 1959. This refuge is managed for ducks, geese and other water birds. Water impoundments equipped with control structures help make this a suitable area for migrating waterfowl using the Atlantic Flyway. Waterfowl using the area include Canada geese, snow geese, whistling swans, pintails, mallards, black ducks and many others.

SOUTH CAROLINA

CAPE ROMAIN, Box 191, Rt. 1, Awendaw, S.C. 29429
Acquisition of this refuge began in 1932. It covers 34,000 acres, primarily for geese, ducks, wild turkeys, shore birds, gulls and terns, as well as sea turtles and alligators. Water levels are frequently manipulated in the six brackish impoundments to control pest plants. Fishing is permitted for

black bass, bluegills and shellcrackers, as well as spot-tail bass, croaker and drum. During one week in December hunting is permitted on the Bulls Island unit of the refuge. Such hunting is limited to the use of bow and arrow for whitetail deer, squirrels and raccoons. Camping is permitted only during the archery hunts. The bird list totals 268 species. The Bulls Island unit is famous for its unspoiled subtropical beauty. Dominick House, concession-operated, offers meals and comfortable lodging.

CAROLINA SANDHILLS, Box 130, Rt. 2, McBee, S.C. 29101
This refuge of 45,000 acres was acquired in 1939. Canada geese and sixteen species of ducks winter here. Most common among them are the mallards, black ducks, ringnecks and wood ducks. There are also good populations of wild turkeys, bobwhites and whitetail deer. Fishing is permitted for black bass, bluegill and catfish from mid-March to mid-October. Deer hunting is by permit only, in keeping with state regulations. Camping is limited to group camping by permit. Bird watchers have recorded 190 species on this refuge.

SANTEE, Box 158, Summerton, S.C. 29148
In 1941 this refuge of 74,000 acres was set aside for geese, ducks and herons. At that time waterfowl numbered only a few hundred a year during the winter. Today 30,000 Canada geese spend the winter here with 85,000 ducks. Fishermen come to catch black bass, white bass, striped bass, crappie, perch, bream and catfish. There is no hunting or camping. The bird list includes 208 species.

SOUTH DAKOTA

LACREEK, Martin, S.D. 57551
Established in 1935, this 16,100-acre refuge is of prime importance to Central Flyway waterfowl. Eleven pool and marsh impoundments, formed by a system of dikes, provide 5000 acres of waterfowl habitat ranging from deep open water to shallow water producing emergent vegetation. Blue-winged teal and mallards are common nesting birds. There is also a wide variety of other waterfowl and

shore birds and a nesting colony of pelicans and cormorants. On this refuge, in 1963, trumpeter swans nested successfully east of the Rocky Mountains for the first time in eighty years. The bird list contains 225 species.

SAND LAKE, Columbia, S.D. 57433
Sand Lake was purchased in 1935. It contains 21,459 acres, and provides protection and ample food for geese, ducks, pheasants and sharp-tailed grouse. Between 200,000 and 500,000 geese stop here in spring and attract large crowds of people. Again in the fall some 400,000 ducks and 100,000 geese stop in to rest and feed on their way south. Two dikes have been constructed to flood large areas of the refuge with water from one to three feet deep. In these areas grow luxuriant stands of phragmites, cattails and bulrushes, which provide habitat for ducks. Over this refuge are scattered shelter-belt trees, marshes, open impoundments and mixed prairie grassland, as well as some cultivated fields. The area is highly popular with photographers and bird watchers. The refuge bird list numbers more than 225 species.

WAUBAY, Waubay, S.D. 57273
Ducks and geese make good use of this 4650-acre refuge established in 1935 as a link in the chain of waterfowl refuges along the Central Flyway. The major aim is to preserve wetlands for waterfowl. Canada geese are once again nesting in the refuge. This breeding flock had its beginning in 1937 with thirty geese that had been used as hunting decoys. Goose-nesting islands are constructed by refuge personnel to give the birds isolation and cut down predation. Potholes are enlarged and deepened. Additional habitat is created by building dikes to impound water. Public use of this refuge is limited. The bird list includes 230 species.

TENNESSEE

REELFOOT, Box 295, Samburg, Tenn. 38254
This refuge, on a part of the historic Reelfoot Lake, contains about 9500 acres. The refuge was established in

1941, under an agreement with the State of Tennessee, primarily as a waterfowl area. Reelfoot is a famed fishing lake for bass, crappie and bluegills. There is no hunting. Management practices include a farming program to provide food for geese and ducks. In recent years the area has developed as a wintering refuge for Canada geese; 20,000 or more now spend the winter. Extensive work is also carried out in the control of undesirable vegetation to improve waterfowl habitat. This is a primitive and beautiful lake rimmed by great cypress trees. Shore and wading birds, as well as many kinds of reptiles and amphibians, live here in abundance. The bird list contains 230 species.

TENNESSEE, Box 849, Paris, Tenn. 38242
This refuge of 51,300 acres was created in 1945 on Tennessee Valley Authority lands, for ducks, geese, herons, deer and wild turkeys. Management practices are largely to provide better habitat for waterfowl. The wintering waterfowl populations have climbed to 300,000 ducks and 20,000 geese. On this area fishermen catch crappie, bass, catfish, perch and yellow bass. There is an annual managed deer hunt. The refuge bird list contains 211 species.

TEXAS

ARANSAS, Box 68, Austwell, Tex. 77950

BUFFALO LAKES, Box 228, Umbarger, Tex. 79091
This refuge, acquired by the Fish and Wildlife Service in 1946 for geese and ducks, covers 7664 acres in the Texas Panhandle thirty-two miles southwest of Amarillo. Winter populations occasionally reach one million ducks, largely mallards. Canada geese may number twenty thousand. There is no hunting. Mainly during the summer months when waterfowl use is low, large numbers of people visit the refuge to picnic, fish and water ski.

HAGERMAN, Rte. 3, Box 123, Sherman, Tex. 75090
Established in 1946, this area of 11,320 acres is important to ducks and geese as well as shore birds and wading birds. Primarily it is intended as a feeding and resting area for

migrating and wintering waterfowl using the Central Flyway. More than 100,000 waterfowl, ducks and geese now
use this refuge in the fall. Fishing is permitted from April
through September.

LAGUNA ATASCOSA, Box 2683, Harlingen, Tex. 78550
Great flocks of ducks, geese, shore birds and wading
birds make use of this 45,000-acre refuge. Its acquisition
was begun in 1946. A great variety of birds funnel through
this area during migrations. The annual Christmas bird
count always ranks among the highest in the nation. The
refuge bird list totals 317 species. Primitive camping is
permitted for periods up to three days. There is no hunting. Saltwater fishing as well as boating are available on
the Harlingen arm of the Intracoastal Canal, which cuts
through the northern part of the refuge.

MULESHOE, Box 549, Muleshoe, Tex. 79347
This refuge, acquired in 1939, provides protection for
Canada geese, ducks, sand-hill cranes and shore birds on
its 5800 acres. It is chiefly a wintering area for migratory
waterfowl. Here on the high plains of west Texas the
elevation is 3750 feet above sea level. Grain sorghums and
wheat are grown for wildlife. By August, migrating waterfowl are already arriving at Muleshoe. Sometimes their
numbers reach peak levels of more than 700,000 birds
by the end of the year. Predominant among them are the
pintails, blue-winged teal, American widgeons, mallards,
shovelers, scaups, buffleheads and ruddy ducks. Here, too,
is an outstanding wintering population of the lesser sand-
hill crane, which sometimes numbers more than 50,000
birds on this refuge alone, the largest concentration of
sand-hill cranes in the United States. Almost without fail
they arrive in the third week of September from their
breeding grounds in the arctic. The refuge bird list totals
more than 180 species. Picnics are permitted, but fishing is
limited to one small lake in summertime.

SANTA ANA, Alamo, Tex. 78516
This bird watcher's paradise on the Texas-Mexico border
lies in a bend of the Rio Grande and covers 2000 acres.
Some of the 272 species of birds recorded here are found

nowhere else in the United States. The refuge, a jungle-like forest of native trees, preserves a type of lowland forest that has largely disappeared from the region. No fires or camping are permitted.

UTAH

BEAR RIVER MIGRATORY BIRD REFUGE, Box 548, Brigham City, Utah 84302
This refuge, containing 64,895 acres, was established in 1928 for whistling swans, Canada geese, ducks, grebes, white pelicans and shore birds. The refuge headquarters is fifteen miles west of Brigham City. It is one of the nation's outstanding waterfowl nesting and feeding areas. During peak migration periods spectacular flocks of ducks assemble here. The refuge contains five large pools on which water levels can be regulated. Visitors may take the twelve-mile drive around one of these areas on a gravel road. Among the nesting birds are large numbers of egrets, herons, ibises and shore birds. Some 45,000 ducklings and 2500 goslings are produced on this refuge each year. There are times in the early fall when it may be host to a million ducks. Pintails predominate, and green-winged teal, American widgeons, mallards, redheads and shovelers occur in great abundance. In season a part of this refuge is open to waterfowl hunting. Fishing is permitted on certain parts.

FISH SPRINGS, Dugway, Utah 84022
This 17,900-acre refuge is a natural marsh which gets its water supply from permanent springs. The refuge was established in 1959 for the benefit of nesting and migrating waterfowl. Once a pony express station and an overland stagecoach stop, this refuge is now isolated and reached mainly by dirt road. Future developments will create more open water for waterfowl. Primitive camping is permitted on the refuge.

OURAY, Box 398, Vernal, Utah 84078
Ouray was established in 1960 for Canada geese, ducks, wading birds and shore birds. It will contain 11,200 acres

when acquisition is completed. The purpose of this refuge
is to provide nesting habitat, as well as food and protection, for migrating waterfowl, including the Great Basin
Canada goose.

VERMONT

MISSISQUOI, Swanton, Vt. 05488
This refuge was established in 1948. It covers 4600 acres
for the protection of Canada geese and ducks. Situated
forty miles north of Burlington, Vermont, the refuge terrain is river-delta flood plains composed of open marsh,
wooded swamp and ponds. Management is aimed at re-
taining the area as wetland. There is fishing for walleye,
pike, bass and bullheads around the refuge but not in the
interior part, where human traffic would disturb nesting
waterfowl. The bird list for this refuge includes 185
species.

VIRGINIA

BACK BAY, Box 6128, Virginia Beach, Va. 23456
This refuge, twenty-five miles southeast of Norfolk, was
purchased in 1938 to protect whistling swans, geese, ducks
and shore birds. It includes 4600 acres, about half of
which is open water. The remainder is marshlands and
sand dunes. The area is popular for bird watching and fishing. About 250 species of birds have been recorded here.
Among the most numerous are snow geese, Canada geese,
mallards, green-winged teal, American widgeons, scaups,
canvasbacks, redheads and ruddy ducks. This is also a
great gathering place for whistling swans. Refuge headquarters can be reached only by four-wheel-drive vehicles
along the beach.

CHINCOTEAGUE, Box 62, Chincoteague, Va. 23336
Greater snow geese, brant, ducks and shore birds come
to this 9000-acre refuge in large numbers. This refuge
was purchased in 1943. Typical of the barrier islands
found along the Atlantic Coast, it has a wide sandy beach

behind which are low dunes. Farther inland are broad salt marshes, fresh-water pools and cultivated fields. A major refuge management problem is stabilizing the dunes to keep salt water from flooding fresh-water areas. The lower four miles of the refuge have been set aside as a recreation area, used by many people for swimming, picnicking and surf fishing.

PRESQUILE, Box 658, Hopewell, Va. 23860
Presquile was given to the government in 1952 for a duck and goose refuge. It is an island of 1329 acres created when a navigation channel, cut across the James River, turned an old oxbow bend into a true island. Canada geese winter here in great numbers. There are also a few blue geese and snow geese. The bird list contains nearly 200 species. Visitors may reach Presquile by a government-operated ferry from the mainland.

WASHINGTON

COLUMBIA, Othello, Wash. 99344
Established in 1944, this waterfowl refuge now contains 28,900 acres. This is one of the most important newer refuges in the Pacific Flyway. Located in the heart of the Columbia Basin Reclamation Project, it will eventually contain 33,000 acres. Within it will be five developed marsh units and a number of lakes, as well as 1500 acres of irrigated cropland to provide food for migrant and wintering waterfowl. Mallards and Canada geese winter here in large numbers. There is fishing for rainbow trout and also hunting for pheasants and waterfowl. The public hunting area covers some 7500 acres of the refuge. Camping is permitted in designated areas in conjunction with hunting and fishing. The refuge bird list contains 183 species. Headquarters is in the city of Othello.

MCNARY, Box 19, Burbank, Wash. 99323
Acquired in 1955, this waterfowl refuge covers 3300 acres. Farming of 900 acres for grains and millet supplements the 700 acres of natural marsh and aquatic vegetation. These practices have brought great increases to the water-

fowl populations. This refuge is primarily a resting and feeding area for migrating waterfowl. Recreation use is limited to fishing for warm-water species. The manager of this refuge also administers the nearby Cold Springs and McKay Creek national wildlife refuges in Oregon. These are both waterfowl refuges superimposed on reclamation reservoirs.

TURNBULL, Rte. 3, Box 107, Cheney, Wash. 99004
Established in 1937, this refuge covers 17,200 acres and provides protection for Great Basin Canada geese, ducks, ruffed grouse, California quail and shore birds. Major management practices here are cultivation of 200 acres of cereal grains for migratory waterfowl, grassland management, timber management and the control of water levels in marshlands. There is no fishing or hunting. Camping is restricted to organized groups by permit. The bird list includes 180 species.

WILLAPA, Ilwaco, Wash. 98624
Purchased in 1937 for black brant, Canada geese and other waterfowl, this refuge covers 9600 acres. It is a major wintering area for black brant. There is waterfowl hunting and archery hunting for deer and bear as conditions permit. The manager of this refuge is also responsible for administration of a number of offshore colonial-sea-bird nesting islands in Oregon and Washington. These islands make up the Oregon Islands and Three Arch Rocks national wildlife refuges off the coast of Oregon; the Copalis, Flattery Rocks, and Quillayute Needles national wildlife refuges off the coast of Washington; and the Jones Island, Matia Island, San Juan and Smith Island national wildlife refuges in Puget Sound. Nesting here are puffins, murres, pelagic cormorants, gulls, guillemots, petrels and auklets. In addition to these islands, the Cape Meares National Wildlife Refuge in Oregon, and the Dungeness National Wildlife Refuge in Washington are also administered from Willapa.

WISCONSIN

HORICON, Rte. 2, Mayville, Wis. 53050

NECEDAH, Necedah, Wis. 54646
This refuge covers 39,600 acres. It was established in 1939 and since then has become exceedingly successful as an area for Canada geese and other waterfowl. Refuge headquarters is seven miles west of Necedah. This refuge is characterized by many ponds and marshes, separated by sandy ridges. Jack pine grows here, along with oak, aspen, willow and white and red pine. The captive goose flock here was initiated in 1939. The bird list on Necedah includes more than 200 species. Among the summer residents are sand-hill cranes. Fishing is permitted from early July to mid-September. This is the period between nesting and heavy use by migrant birds in the fall. The fish taken include northern pike and bullheads.

WYOMING

HUTTON LAKE, Box 457, Walden, Colo. 81144
This refuge, covering 1968 acres, was set aside in 1932, largely for the use of waterfowl and shore birds. It offers no recreational facilities.

NATIONAL ELK REFUGE, Box C, Jackson, Wyo. 83001

Index